NAKED CONSUMPTION

Naked Consumption

Retail Trends Uncovered

Second Edition

Anthony J. Stokan

Anthony Russell Inc.

Toronto, Canada

Published by
Anthony Russell Inc.
300 Bloor Street East, Suite 1906, Toronto, Canada M4W 3Y2

Printed by
RJ Communications LLC
51 East 42nd Street, Suite 1202, New York, NY 10017

Cover design
Duncan Aitken

Interior design and layout
Budget Book Design.com

Back cover portraits
Ola Sirant

Cover photography
Anthony J. Stokan

ISBN: 0-9737819-0-4 (paperback)
Printed in the United States of America
This is an Anthony Russell Inc. book.

CONTENTS

ACKNOWLEDGEMENTS

I'D like to thank everyone who helped create the second edition of *Naked Consumption.*

Duncan Aitken – a passionate and creative designer, who conceived the perfect cover within minutes.

Cameron Groves – my gifted wordsperson, who grasps every idea and thought I present, and has the extraordinary ability to connect and distil what matters.

Russell Connolly – a special thank you to my partner, soul mate and constant intellectual companion – my first editor, critic and all-round supporter. Sharing ideas with him is one of the great joys of my life.

Anthony J. Stokan
Toronto, Fall 2008

I dedicate this book to the hundreds of clients and audiences in Canada, the United States, Mexico, Ecuador, Chile, Brazil, the United Kingdom, France, Germany, Spain, Turkey, Oman, the United Arab Emirates and South Africa who have embraced my ideas about marketing, research and consumer behaviour. It has been a pleasure to work with so many passionate, dedicated individuals. They have enabled me to experience how seamless the world is, and how rewarding it is to communicate my ideas and adapt them to unique situations around the globe.

I have had the privilege of sharing my observations on consumer behaviour and trends for the past two decades, as I have anchored more than 1,000 conferences and management meetings worldwide. I am committed to building a rapport with every audience I address, offering examples they can relate to and providing relevant, actionable insights. Nothing is more rewarding than standing in front of a room of a hundred or a thousand professionals and taking part in the creative process of developing new ideas that will move our industry forward.

INTRODUCTION

THE GOODS ON RETAIL

TO save, or to consume? This question has haunted consumers throughout our world of hyper-consumption for more than a decade now. The overwhelming impression is that we are living way beyond our means, and seemingly unable to save ourselves from wanting – and spending – more.

This book is the result of watching consumers consume during the past two decades, observing the fascinating way they behave in stores, and how they go about making purchases. During that time my partner Russell and I have conducted dozens of shopping centre intercept projects, and facilitated dozens of focus groups with the household CEO – the primary shopper most often referred to as Mom. We have always been fascinated with how and why consumers consume and how they deal with money, especially their own.

What have we learned from all this? That consumers – you, me and just about everyone else – are, well, weird about money. At restaurants, for instance, we tip less on rainy days, and more when we eat alone. We tip more generously when the server draw a smiley face on the bill. (This makes you wonder whether Wally World's bouncy happy face has similar persuasive powers.)

Did you know half of all consumers lose sleep at least once per week because of money worries? Almost a quarter of us count how much money we have in our wallet at least once a day. Three quarters of us stash our cash in strictly regimented order, with bills arranged from small to large. Only one in three of us feels in control of our money. Almost half feel guilt about overspending at least once a month. And did you know Canadians lead the planet in debit card use?

There are plenty of surprises when you look at how people spend their money – and, in particular, how they approach shopping.

What I have set out to do with this book is throw light on how we experience retail, and how we are likely to experience it in the future based on current trends. *Naked Consumption* looks at the dynamics of a new retail landscape, where consumers call the shots. From the big box to e-commerce to fast fashion to new luxury, the book aims to expose the key trends that retailers and shopping centres will need to grapple with in the years ahead.

Naked Consumption deals with crucial issues affecting consumers, retailers and shopping centres, including declining customer loyalty, the dominance of Wal-Mart, and the brilliant branding of stores like Zara, Starbucks and Ikea. I hope each of the ten chapters will give you some new insight into how shoppers shop, and how sellers sell.

In these times of tumultuous change, it is absolutely crucial for retailers and shopping centres to find new ways to deliver superior shopping experiences to customers. The retail landscape of the future will demand nothing less.

CHAPTER 1

THE DEATH OF INSPIRATION

THE JOYS OF SHOPPING

THERE'S much more to shopping than buying things. From the bustling agora of ancient Athens to the opulent arcades of 19th-century Paris, London and Milan, people have always loved browsing and being entertained in colourful public spaces. Far more than a commercial activity, shopping is one of the most vital components of the communities we live in.

Yet some of the world's most successful retailers seem to have lost sight of those enjoyable aspects of shopping that have no direct impact on their bottom line. The success of discounters like Wal-Mart and warehouse format stores like Costco shows that consumers willingly forego many shopping pleasures to get things at better prices.

This focus on delivering goods for less plays a key role in transforming much shopping into an uninspired chore. Big box retailers depend on advanced manufacturing and supply chain technologies to reduce costs. With their harsh lighting, endless aisles and vast parking lots, they sacrifice almost everything that makes shopping enjoyable in the name of price cutting. Since getting a bargain is always in vogue, many consumers willingly trade customer service and entertainment value for savings.

By contrast, the great retailers of a century ago made architecturally magnificent stores, sumptuous displays, elegant dining and professional service integral parts of department store shopping.

It's hard to see the rise of the big box as a positive development, when in most ways it represents the decline of many of the joys of shopping. At the same time, waxing nostalgic about a lost golden era won't lead to better sales for retailers, nor will it create more satisfying experiences for shoppers.

Yet in this age of discounting there's still a place for retailers and shopping centres that engage shoppers' imaginations. Cost cutting is not the only route to providing more customer satisfaction. Because retailers are able to match the competition on price and merchandise selection almost instantaneously these days, creativity and inspiration are more important than ever.

Many consumers are spending less time shopping because they find it a chore. This is why retailers need to look beyond their bottom line for fresh ideas that will bring the fun back to shopping.

Department Stores: Rise and Fall

Modern retail begins with the department store, a style of retail that has been losing ground to other formats for over half a century. Recent decades have seen a number of legendary department stores close their doors for good, including beloved chains such as Wanamaker's in the U.S. and Eaton's in Canada. Some surviving chains continue to struggle to assert their relevance, while others have reinvented themselves to become more exciting destinations than ever.

The first department store, the Bon Marché in Paris, opened its doors in 1852. It offered shoppers the novelty of a wide range of merchandise – from fashion to sporting goods to furniture – under one roof.

The department store provided urbanites the opportunity to combine shopping with entertainment. Nineteenth-century consumers could plan a whole day around exploring the products and experiences brought together in magnificent department stores like A.T. Stewart in New York, Liberty & Co. in London and Marshall Field's in Chicago. There was nothing unusual about whiling away an afternoon browsing the abundance of merchandise showcased in these grand temples of consumption.

By the 1870s, the names of leading department stores had become widely recognized brands. Downtown locations served them well, thanks to the transportation systems of the day: the car would not become ubiquitous for another half-century. The only competition for this new kind of retailing was the mom-and-pop store.

One of the most important developments the department store brought to retail was a permanent change in the nature of transactions. Phrases such as "Goods satisfactory or your money refunded" had never been heard before.

Department stores' fixed prices were also novel. As places that aimed to entertain while purveying merchandise, department stores actually worked to keep people's minds off prices, aiming to immerse customers fully in the shopping experience.

In our own price-obsessed era, people focus much of their shopping energy on looking for the best deal, often at the expense of other pleasurable aspects of shopping. In some ways this recalls the bad old days before the department store tycoons revolutionized retail and showed us how much fun shopping could be.

As department stores' popularity grew, they became woven into society's fabric. In New York, Wanamaker's featured an art gallery and an entrance hall, transforming the store from a place where women bought things into a social institution. Wanamaker's Philadelphia flagship, rebranded as a Lord & Taylor in the mid-'90s, developed Christmas window displays that became such an integral part of the city's festivities that the program continues today, despite changes in management.

In Toronto, Eaton's art deco flagship opened with great fanfare in the 1920s. It was crowned by a concert hall, which the company boasted was one of the finest on the continent. Though the restored auditorium is once again hosting events, the main level of the store, a soaring space clad in travertine, is occupied by discounter Winners.

A number of the department stores that continue to thrive, such as New York icons Bergdorf Goodman and Barneys, have positioned themselves as upscale clothing stores offering secondary lines in cosmetics and home décor items. These stores are in business today partly because they preserve something of the excitement of traditional department store shopping.

Another survivor, Bloomingdale's, has brought excitement to shopping by orchestrating events such as flying in *fraises des bois* (tiny wild strawberries prized for their flavour) to its gourmet shops. While this generates traffic, it has never been a money-maker for the retailer. Yet it's precisely efforts like this, whose impact on the bottom line may be intangible, that make institutions of what would otherwise be merely stores. People are more likely to feel loyal to retailers that host one-of-a-kind events that they enjoy.

The decline of department stores is linked to the appearance of the first suburban shopping malls in the '50s. Their decline has also coincided with a psychological shift in North American attitudes toward institutions. In recent decades, institutions such as churches and corporations have been wracked by scandal. Consumers are understandably skeptical that profit-driven retailers could have their best interests at heart.

The increased cynicism of modern society has been a problem for department stores, because these retailers built their business on trust. The money-back guarantee was conceived to engender trust in customers, as was the notion of making everything available under one roof. Once upon a time, department stores were places where consumers could be sure they would find just about everything they needed – and where they could easily return it if necessary.

In recent decades, department stores have eliminated unprofitable departments in the struggle for survival. Yet many of these unprofitable areas were an integral part of what made the department store what it once was, and an important part of what made people trust the stores and become loyal customers.

WINDOW WONDERLAND

One element of department store culture that has faded along with the stores themselves is the art of window dressing. Salvador Dali and Andy Warhol both held posts as window dressers in the department store's 20th-century heyday; other legends in the field include Gene Moore, who decorated Tiffany's iconic windows from 1955 to 1995, and the rebellious Candy Pratts Price of Bloomingdale's.

Simon Doonan, creative director of Barneys in New York, is a contemporary practitioner of this dying art. He makes use of celebrity likenesses and current events references to create what he calls "crazy bits of street theatre." Barneys' witty windows are one of the store's most potent ways of reinforcing its unique brand, combining notions of luxury and taste with a sense of humour. Doonan's innovative creations have been held up as prime examples of contemporary department store culture, and have played a significant role in helping Barneys reinforce its relevance in the marketplace.

Retailers like H&M and Gap use mass-produced window packages that can easily be installed by store managers the world over, but critics of standardization maintain that unique and striking store windows continue to serve an important purpose. A good window display differentiates the retailer, engaging people's imaginations and creating positive associations with the store, ultimately giving shoppers a reason not to go elsewhere.

Going Corporate

Changes in the definitions of certain department store jobs have played a role in these retailers' decline. Window dressing, for instance, has in many stores become a management position, more than a purely creative one.

The stores' buyers have also seen their role diminished. Whereas there was once considerable prestige attached to buying fashions for the big department stores, the position of buyer is now merely a stop on the way to a corporate position. Buying is increasingly done on the corporate level.

What this means is that department stores are not as good as they once were at supplying fashions that reflect their customers' lives. Once upon a time, buyers in some stores knew their clientele personally, so the fashions sold mirrored customers' tastes. These days, there are few department stores where consumers expect to find a fashion selection that suits them personally – another example of how corporate cost cutting can make shopping less compelling.

Give the Lady What She Wants

Marshall Field, founder of the Chicago store of the same name, famously pronounced, "Give the lady what she wants." This strikingly modern perspective reflects the great retailer's understanding that the number one job of any retailer is to meet and exceed customers' expectations.

Many department stores stopped giving customers what they want long ago, and have either folded or lost market share as a result. Even venerable Marshall Fields was acquired by Macy's, which dispensed with the Marshall Fields name even at the Chicago flagship, much to the chagrin of the store's devoted following. But retailers that have adapted to the new business landscape while preserving the best of the department store experience show there's still life in the old format.

Selfridges, in the U.K., is a business that has conspicuously embraced a fresh approach to department store retailing – with conspicuously positive results. The department store chain's former chief executive, Italian-born

Vittorio Radice, received most of the credit for transforming the retailer from a sleepy '70s-style department store dinosaur into the retailer most synonymous with cool among London's young and hip.

According to the new model, more floor space is rented to vendors, who design their own booths and are encouraged to be creative. The store also hosts excitement-generating events, some of which bring significant edge to the department store experience. For example, Selfridges hosted an event called Body Craze, where 500 naked people rode the store's escalators as part of an installation by New York artist Spencer Tunick.

The new Selfridges aims to create a shopping experience that is interesting and unique – not unlike the old department stores at their creative best. The retailer's management is keenly aware that it is competing for shoppers' leisure time as well as their disposable income, and aims to keep them entertained.

The excitement generated by Selfridges inspired Marshall Fields to revamp its Chicago flagship, setting aside ten per cent of its selling space for unique shops and boutiques. An increased focus on brands and on the needs of younger shoppers is intended to reinforce the store's relevance.

Clearly the industry-wide emphasis on price-cutting at the expense of the fun aspects of shopping creates significant opportunities for those willing to get creative. Innovative retailers have successfully transformed their stores into exciting – not to mention highly profitable – destinations, just like the great department stores of yesteryear. Imagination is still valuable in an industry obsessed with the bottom line.

LIFESTORE: STYLE IS NOT ENOUGH

Like many old-guard retailers at the dawn of the 21st century, the U.K.'s Marks & Spencer found itself saddled with a less-than-sexy image. That's why the 120-year-old department store chain hired Vittorio Radice away from Selfridges in 2002. Well known for his successful makeovers of other British stores, it was hoped Radice would modernize the M&S brand and reverse declining revenues. His first big M&S project was a housewares and furniture emporium called Lifestore.

At Lifestore's grand opening Radice said, "We must be the biggest seller of G-strings in the world and we should be proud of it." This ambition was at odds with the chain's real place in the retail landscape: despite its frumpy image, M&S was still Britain's largest supplier of pants and socks.

What Radice meant, of course, was that the Marks & Spencer brand needed sexing up. Lifestore was an ambitious step in that direction.

A Fresh Concept

Radice's plans for the old British chain reflected a wider trend: the middle market's increasing taste for affordable luxury. Declining profits indicated M&S had been doing a poor job of responding to this new consumer zeitgeist.

At Radice's urging, M&S agreed to invest £15 million in Lifestore's dazzling pilot location in Gateshead, in northeast England. From its architecture to its merchandise to its discreet black and white logo, Lifestore was a dramatic departure from the dowdy image most shoppers associated with Marks & Spencer. At the heart of the new store was a freestanding two-storey house designed by minimalist architect and lifestyle guru John Pawson.

There was little conventional signage, because customers were expected to discover the store's sections on their own. There were no departments in the usual sense, but rather concepts, such as Relax, Cook, and Celebrate, featuring items for every kind of entertaining. Storage and desks were available in the section called Organise, while Rest, Relax, Renew, Escape and Alfresco provided an array of indoor and outdoor possibilities.

Radice had help with the concept. It originated with the previous M&S homewares division team, and he brought in a couple of big names to add some pizzazz. Canadian Tyler Brûlé, the creative force behind *Wallpaper** magazine, handled the graphic presentation, designing a catalogue that epitomized lifestyle chic. Ilse Crawford of *Elle Decoration* was responsible for the overall appearance of the house-within-a-store, making it look as if people really lived there.

Lifestore's polished concrete floors and subtle lighting set off an eclectic mix of furniture, lighting, linens, ceramics and glassware. Radice edited Marks & Spencer's previous collection of housewares and introduced 1,200 new products, such as stacking white bone-china cups and saucers, and boomerang-backed dining chairs. Lifestore was a cornucopia of early 21st-century modernity.

Some pricing was intended to appeal to the traditional M&S shopper. For instance, there were plates priced at £2, and glasses for 50p. These were displayed alongside high-design items like a red leather sectional sofa priced at £4,998.

For those who couldn't make the trek to the store there was the Lifestore website: about 3,000 of the store's 12,000 products could be bought online. A slick catalogue dubbed the Marks & Spencer Design Directory offered about 2,200 items.

Faced with slow sales even in the first couple of weeks, Radice conceded the prices would need fine-tuning. Younger customers commented ominously they could find the same stuff cheaper at Ikea.

The Bottom Line

Although lauded in the British press for its appealing merchandise and design sense, Lifestore had its share of critics. One writer pointed out that both Tyler Brûlé and John Pawson were figures from the nineties rather than the new decade, and the minimalism they championed was already waning.

Retail analysts questioned Radice's handling of the Marks & Spencer brand. Not all members of the retailer's board were pleased he had challenged the M&S status quo by calling for extra fitting rooms to separate young, lean women customers from the matronly ladies who made up M & S's core clientele.

Others said Lifestore could do little to reverse the chain's fortunes, given that home furnishings accounted for only £500 million of its £8 billion annual sales. Just two more Lifestore openings were planned for the 18 months following the launch, limiting the concept's potential to boost the bottom line. (M&S initially said it would roll out as many as 20 Lifestores over five years.)

Some questioned the store's location. Gateshead, facing Newcastle across the river Tyne, is 400 km north of London, not far from the Scottish border. It is ostensibly a community on the up and up, with growing numbers of affluent young professionals escaping England's overpriced southeast to settle there. It's worth noting that the decision to start in Gateshead instead of London was made not by Radice but by his predecessor at M&S.

Sales in the first few months were slow: the *Financial Times* reported they were running more than 10 per cent below target. The *Guardian* reported Lifestore's sales were so dismal that insiders had taken to calling it Deathstore.

In June 2004, four months into Lifestore's short life, Vittorio Radice was ousted from his post and given a generous severance package. In July, Marks

& Spencer was confronted with an attempted takeover by a consortium of investors. The retailer announced a recovery plan that involved closing the Gateshead store and abandoning the Lifestore concept.

In January 2005, M & S entered into a deal with Danish furniture retailer ILVA to sell the Gateshead Lifestore site for an estimated £35 million. The John Pawson house that served as the store's centerpiece was to be removed to make way for the new occupant's more utilitarian style of retail.

With Lifestore Radice had set out to change the way people thought about Marks & Spencer. Traffic numbers had in fact been healthy, indicating he partly succeeded. But more customers needed to walk away with purchases for this aesthetic triumph to be a commercial success. Some lamented the fact that Lifestore was given only a few months to turn a profit, whereas Selfridges' bottom line didn't improve until three years after Radice's makeover.

Marks & Spencer's decision to hire Radice had been motivated by a situation faced by many retailers: how to maintain market share in the face of aggressively efficient new competition? Well-established stores in search of new relevance face the challenge of hanging onto core customers while modernizing their image to bring in new business. Predicting which changes will attract new customers and which will drive old ones away can be tricky in a constantly changing marketplace.

Cheap Chic

The department store's decline can be traced to some of the same forces that have transformed the fashion industry. The department store was born in an era when things moved more slowly, and when the latest styles cost more than the clothes on the racks of down-market retailers.

These days, consumers looking for the very latest check out stores like H&M and Zara, where style is available at throwaway prices. Well-heeled shoppers in search of luxury items drop into Target or other discounters of branded merchandise, where luxury goods are available at affordable prices every day.

Shoppers have become reluctant to pay extra for some luxuries, as many distinctions between high-end and low-end goods are disappearing. Luxury materials such as cashmere, for instance, are now available at bargain prices. In the department store's heyday, consumers were willing to pay a premium for cashmere. They were also much more likely to believe their favourite store's brand was a guarantee that they were getting their money's worth.

Fashion itself was different then, too. A few decades ago, fashion brands were set apart by both quality and creativity. People paid high prices for clothes bearing designer labels because that meant the clothes were well-made, and designed by someone with a unique sense of style, not to mention insight into fashion trends. Just as important, the clothes could not be found elsewhere for less.

It used to be that department stores were something like clubs. Shopping at them implied a set of values shared with other customers, especially if the store was perceived as "exclusive." The top designer names were worn by a select few, and wearing them was a means of being recognized and approved of by others in the same club.

These days, haute-luxe items – the Louis Vuitton handbag and the Burberry scarf are two examples – are largely ubiquitous. Whether because of the thriving industry in knock-offs or the ready availability of cheap credit, it seems such status symbols are within the reach of almost anyone.

As discussed in the Luxury for All chapter, the best-known makers of status goods have accelerated the democratization of the high life by producing "new luxury" items, placing formerly unaffordable brands within the reach of the masses. If you can't afford Armani, there's always Armani Exchange.

The trouble now is that many feel it may not be worth buying things that everyone already has. People are increasingly skeptical that luxury brands provide the value implied by the price tag. The caveat "All you're paying for is the label" is more widely heeded than ever before.

Consumers these days are savvy and demanding. With easy access via the Internet to information on virtually anything that can be bought or sold, they are less likely to put their trust in a retailer, and less inclined to pay a premium for an item because of its brand.

In other words, if there's nothing special about the item you're buying, there need be nothing special about the place you buy it, beyond a guarantee of lowest price. While the majority of consumers may not love big box shopping, they do love getting a bargain. Faced with price transparency, only retailers that can truly bring something unique to the shopping experience can hope to survive in a landscape cluttered with giant stores offering the lowest price.

Redefining Cool

The apparent decline in the creative output of the fashion world raises another question: Has "cool" itself gone out of fashion? Observers lament a lack of innovation in current designs, as the fashion industry recycles retro looks pillaged from faded fashion magazines and thrift store bins.

A few small brands still present consumers with a distinctive aesthetic – Comme des Garcons and Yohji Yamamoto, for instance. Designs produced by these companies are difficult and unprofitable to knock off, so their clientele continues to get its money's worth in terms of quality and uniqueness.

But many feel the magic has gone out of fashion, and with it the notion that fashion is cool. From roughly the mid-'80s to the late '90s the fashion industry fascinated the masses with a parade of eccentric and over-the-top styles, catapulting models into superstardom and generating controversy by championing unwholesome looks like heroin chic.

Not so now. The more sober mood of the new century, beginning with 9/11 and bolstered by the war in Iraq and economic uncertainty, has encouraged fashion to reassess its values. The unfortunate result is a dearth of fresh ideas on the racks of clothing retailers.

Technology also plays a significant role in reshaping how fashion is perceived and consumed. Before the Internet became ubiquitous, there was a time lag between the birth of a new look on the streets of Tokyo and its being copied around the world. The editors of fashion magazines still exercised some power to determine what was "in."

Now information flows too quickly for any individual or group of people to pass judgment on what people should be wearing. Shopping magazines like Condé Nast's *Lucky* compete with traditional fashion magazines by presenting fashions in a catalogue-like format, which helps shift the power to make fashion choices to the consumer.

Hipsters vs. Hucksters

Another change in the fashion world has been a creeping shift in advertising from selling products to hawking image. Instead of selling a pair of shoes or a sweater, many brands' ads aim to sell something much less tangible, like coolness or sexiness.

Mainstream marketers have become better than ever at bottling the latest in rebellion and transgression, and seem hip to every nascent trend of note. The Internet makes it easy for marketing spies to plug into youth trends around the globe.

Unfortunately for marketers, featuring a style in mass-market advertising encourages early adopters to move on to the next thing. Teens in particular are turned off by slick ad campaigns.

Just as important, the affordability of new looks at Zara and H&M means that if what you take home in your shopping bag isn't really up-to-the-minute, it doesn't matter much anyway. Fashion mistakes are quickly corrected by another trip to the mall.

The Birth of the Shopping Centre

In its mid-twentieth century heyday, department store shopping was a valued part of the urban experience. But just when these stores were at their peak, along came the suburban mall: a new kind of shopping destination, which unexpectedly ushered in the department store's decline.

It's hard to imagine North America without enclosed shopping centres, but just over half a century ago that's exactly the sort of place it was. An Austrian émigré named Victor Gruen is credited with inventing the mall as we know it.

A man of big ideas, Gruen envisioned an entirely new kind of shopping environment. Until the 1950s, the windows and entrances of shopping centre stores faced onto parking areas and interior walkways. The centre Victor Gruen imagined had an almost utopian quality: it would bring a variety of stores and restaurants together under one roof. For the first time stores would face the inside, while exterior walls remained blank. This enclosed shopping environment would be comfortable year-round: heated in winter, air-conditioned in summer.

In October 1956, Southdale Shopping Center, just outside Minneapolis, opened to great fanfare. It had two department store anchors and seventy-two inline stores, and cost $20 million to build. It had two levels connected by escalators, as well as two-tiered parking. In the middle was a "garden court" with a skylight, towering sculpted trees, a fishpond, a 21-foot cage full of tropical birds and a café.

Journalists from major publications across the U.S., including the *New York Times*, *Life* and *Women's Wear Daily*, were on hand to cover the opening. They raved about what they saw.

Victor Gruen also intended Southdale to be a gathering place for the community. The centre hosted boat shows, fine art exhibitions, charity galas and an episode of the *Truth Or Consequences* game show.

More importantly, Gruen's design was copied by developers across North America and abroad. All shopping centres owe something to Southdale's pioneering design.

Refining the Mall

Shopping centre magnate A. Alfred Taubman had just founded a development firm and opened his own open-air shopping centre when Southdale was built. Gruen inspired him to build an enclosed mall in Hayward, California. Still at the helm of one of the biggest – and arguably the best – shopping centre development firms in the U.S., Taubman is credited with perfecting the mall.

With a singular knack for figuring out what attracts shoppers in droves, Taubman has turned lackluster properties into dazzling destinations for shoppers across the U.S. New Jersey's Mall at Short Hills, for instance, was an abject failure when he acquired it in 1980, with only seven stores still operating. Today it is one of the most successful malls in the country, with an impressive roster of department store anchors: Saks, Macy's, Nordstrom and Neiman Marcus.

Taubman properties owe their success to the shopping centre veteran's faultless understanding of consumer psychology. For instance, the centres make use of "adjacencies" to encourage shoppers to keep spending. High end boutiques like Chanel and Gucci are located near high-end department stores such as Neiman Marcus and Saks, so lovers of upscale fashions can easily hop from one to the next. Gadget stores like Sharper Image and Bose are near one another to facilitate electronics spending sprees.

The centres have two levels, because this means a full circuit of the mall's interior brings you back to where you parked. Doing a full circuit of a three-level centre, on the other hand, will land you at the opposite end of the centre – which is why few shoppers ever venture up to the third level in the first place.

Since people travel down more easily than they travel up, Taubman puts more parking on the upper level. His centres encourage people to keep shopping past dusk by incorporating lights that go on when the sun goes down, preventing nightfall from triggering the instinctive response that it's time to go home.

Taubman recognizes the formula for a shopping centre's success is to have well-run department stores as anchor tenants. With their widely-recognized brand names, broad assortment of cosmetics and heavy advertising, department stores are capable of generating the traffic levels a mall needs. Shopping centres are most profitable when the largest number of department store customers patronize them.

TOWARD THE BIG BOX

Not all shopping centres are as carefully thought out as Taubman's, of course. This is in part because merely building them can be immensely profitable. In 1954 – the same year ground was broken for Southdale – the U.S. government changed tax laws concerning the depreciation of property, making it possible for developers to recoup their investment in a fraction of the time it would have taken previously. This made shopping centres a lucrative investment, and real estate investment companies found themselves awash in funds. What ensued was a continent-wide frenzy of shopping centre construction, which peaked in the 1970s.

Malls sprang up where land was cheapest, on communities' fringes. Often the building or expansion of shopping centres failed to reflect the demographics of the places they were built, contributing to the 21st-century dilemma of retail saturation. Nowadays many retailers must use strategies other than opening new stores, such as turning to overseas markets, to increase their revenues.

Department store anchors believed there was good business to be done by locating in enclosed suburban locations with a gaggle of lesser retailers, but in the end the shopping centre hastened the department store's decline. Specialty retailers benefited from department stores' drawing power, not to mention their advertising. Smaller retailers like Gap found they could thrive in shopping centres, partly by attracting customers that would otherwise have bought their clothes at department stores.

As conceived by Victor Gruen, the shopping centre was a place where people could enjoy the best of other kinds of shopping environments, like the traditional downtown, in climate-controlled comfort. Ironically, malls paved the way for dominant big box retailers like Wal-Mart.

Standalone stores were followed by power centres, which group together several big box stores. The power centre represents a marked evolution away from Victor Gruen's people-friendly vision. It's no accident that one of the more recent trends in shopping centre development is to reproduce the architecturally varied, pedestrian-friendly feel of an old-fashioned shopping district.

The irony of the success of the big box is that it takes shopping back to the days before the comfort of the shopping centre, and provides none of the entertainment value of the old-fashioned department store. Far from a utopian vision, the big box shopping environment is a case of the lowest common denominator becoming a universal standard.

The traditional shopping centre now faces stiff competition from retail formats whose chief advantage is lower prices – especially big box stores and online shopping. If some department stores, like Selfridges, have successfully rejuvenated themselves by making shopping exciting, the mall may well be able to do the same. But regaining the interest of jaded consumers will require nothing short of the reinvention of the enclosed shopping centre.

Creativity in Crisis

Albert Einstein said that imagination is more important than knowledge. That's especially true in today's retail world, where imagination seems to be in short supply. The industry suffers from a conservatism rooted in a concern for the bottom line that often precludes experimenting with new ideas.

Yet few would disagree that business demands constant innovation. Businesses of all kinds thrive on a constant stream of fresh ideas that can produce bottom-line results such as higher productivity and lower costs.

Richard Florida's landmark book *The Rise of the Creative Class* links the prosperity of entire regions to the presence of "Bohemian" artists and a diversity that stimulates creative thinking. He sums up his research findings as follows: "The most successful city-regions anywhere are the ones with a social environment that is open to creativity and diversity of all sorts. The ability to attract creative people in arts and culture, and to be open to people of different ethnic, racial and lifestyle groups, provides distinct advantages to regions in generating innovations, growing and attracting high-technology industries, and spurring economic growth."

New ideas can even change consumer behaviour in a significant way. Websites like eBay and amazon.com are excellent examples of retail innovation, as they have changed the way people shop forever.

But traditional retailers are also capable of innovating in ways that will change consumer behaviour and bring the thrill back to shopping. Beyond the big box there are countless ways to create satisfying shopping experiences. What retailers and shopping centres need to do now is get to work and give fresh ideas a central role in the retail industry.

CHAPTER 2

IT'S A WALLY WALLY WORLD

WORLD'S BIGGEST RETAILER

WAL-MART'S net sales for the fiscal year ended January 31, 2008, were a staggering U.S. $375 billion – roughly equivalent to the GDP of Saudi Arabia.

If Wal-Mart continues growing at its current rate until 2020, its revenues will be U.S.$3.2-trillion, or about the size of China's economy in 2007. If the company's workforce continues growing at the same rate it has since it surpassed Sears as America's biggest retailer in 1990, Wal-Mart will employ 8.2 million people in 2020.

The first Wal-Mart store opened in Rogers, Arkansas, in 1962, the same year Kmart and Target made their debut. In 2002 Wal-Mart surpassed Exxon-Mobil as the world's biggest company ever, accounting for 2.3% of American GNP. In 2003 and 2004 Wal-Mart was named by Fortune magazine as the most admired company in America two years in a row. (It fell to No. 12 on the list in 2005-06, and No. 19 in 2007.)

Though plagued by labour-relations lawsuits, Wal-Mart remains overwhelmingly popular in the U.S. and around the world because it allows people of modest means to buy items that would otherwise be beyond their reach. W. Michael Cox, chief economist of the Federal Reserve Bank of Dallas, told the *New York Times* that "Wal-Mart is the greatest thing that ever happened to low-income Americans. They can stretch their dollars and afford things they otherwise couldn't."

Will Wal-Mart maintain its astonishing growth through the end of the next decade? Developments including societal resistance, new legislation and increasing competition will play a role in reining in the giant's expansion.

Meanwhile, international expansion and Wal-Mart's everyday low prices will draw millions of new customers each year.

BEYOND COMPARE

Wal-Mart Stores Inc. is not only the world's largest retailer but the largest American corporation in terms of sales. A few Wal-Mart facts:

- Wal-Mart is world's largest private employer.
- Over 80 per cent of American households make at least one purchase at Wal-Mart each year.
- Wal-Mart accounts for a tenth of U.S. imports from China.
- Wal-Mart sells more dog food, disposable diapers, guns, toothpaste, CDs and diamonds than any other U.S. retailer.
- It develops more real estate and consumes more energy than any other American company.
- In 21 states Wal-Mart employs more people than the U.S. Army.
- Wal-Mart has its own satellite, used to transmit data on every sale to headquarters in Bentonville.

Some credit Wal-Mart with the impressive productivity gains experienced by the U.S. in the past decade, and analysts often point out that the less affluent are the first to benefit from the company's low prices on basics such as food and clothing. Grocery prices drop an average of thirteen per cent in markets where Wal-Mart has established itself.

Traditionally, companies that monopolize a market raise prices, whereas Wal-Mart lowers them. Until the lawsuits and accusations of sexism, unpaid overtime and employing illegal immigrants started in 2003, Wal-Mart received mostly praise for its astonishingly low prices.

The Wal-Mart formula: buy merchandise at low cost, sell it at rock bottom prices and watch consumers consume voraciously. The company has applied this common-sense formula in ways no other retailer has even attempted.

Wal-Mart International

While securing a growing share of its home market, Wal-Mart is looking to its international operations for continuing exponential growth. For instance, it is now Mexico's largest private employer.

Arriving in Canada in 1994, Wal-Mart quickly surpassed the Hudson's Bay Company to become the country's leading retailer. Discounter Zellers struggled to maintain market share. Wal-Mart grabbed a piece of the Canadian grocery market by offering groceries in both its discount stores and Sam's Club warehouse stores before opening its first Canadian supercenters in 2006.

Wal-Mart is also established in China, Japan, and the United Kingdom, and is overwhelmingly popular in Central and South America, with stores in Argentina, Brazil, Costa Rica, El Salvador, Guatemala, Honduras, Nicaragua and Puerto Rico, in addition to the banners it operates in Mexico. Untapped international markets include India, where the retailer began exploring retail opportunities in 2006.

The discounter's international expansion has not been trouble-free. In Germany Wal-Mart enjoyed some success in changing labour laws and store hours, but had to readjust its objectives as it faced legal snags and was ordered to raise prices, culminating in the 2006 sale of its 85 German stores. Facing conflicts with the retail culture of South Korea, the company opted to sell its 16 stores there the same year.

Secrets of Success

In 2003 Fortune magazine interviewed retail legend Sol Price, founder of Fed-Mart and Price Club. Price said retailing broke down into three main components – personnel, product and facilities – and that the same six rules apply to all three categories.

"You've got to have the right kind, in the right place, at the right time, in the right quantity, in the right condition, at the right price."

No one took these principles to heart more than Sam Walton. In fact, Walton once confessed to Price that Wal-Mart was based on Fed-Mart. Some years later, Walton copied the Price Club model when he established Sam's Club.

Wal-Mart's unmatched command of retailing fundamentals made the company as much a favourite on Wall Street as it is among consumers. Despite bustling checkout lines and crowded parking lots, customers keep coming back because of the everyday low pricing.

- By policy, Wal-Mart aims to keep prices lower than anyone else.
- Frugality characterizes all levels of Wal-Mart's operations: traveling executives share hotel rooms and head office is no-frills, utilitarian building in a low-rent location.
- Buying in volume is only part of Wal-Mart's formula for driving down prices.
- Suppliers are eager to reduce their margins substantially to sell to Wal-Mart and fulfill its volume demands.
- Relentless cost reduction at the store level plays a significant role in the Wal-Mart advantage.

Sam Walton's mantra:

Stack it deep
Sell it cheap
Stack it high and watch it fly
Hear those downtown merchants cry!

Welcome to Wal-Mart

Wal-Mart claims the three principles of its company culture are respect for the individual, service to customers and striving for excellence.

The retailer's greeters play an important role in creating the impression that Wal-Mart cares, warming shoppers up with a simple "Hello" or "How are you today?" This effort to counteract the depersonalization of shopping is being copied across the U.S., with businesses as diverse as Abercrombie & Fitch, Old Navy, Home Depot and Bloomingdale's introducing greeters to their stores.

Media and Transportation

More than any retailer in the world, Wal-Mart uses technology to achieve productivity that outpaces the competition.

Wal-Mart has its own closed-circuit TV network. Entertaining programming is complemented by shows hosted by executives that focus on certain regions or job functions.

Premier Retail Networks (PRN) operates the network in Wal-Mart's discount stores and Sam's Clubs. Ad time is sold to companies that sell products in the stores, such as Unilever and Procter & Gamble.

It is estimated that more than one-third of American shoppers visit Wal-Mart once a week, and half go once a month. This gives PRN's Wal-Mart network greater reach than any network apart from NBC, CBS, ABC and Fox.

According to Nielsen, the average Wal-Mart shopper soaks up five minutes of Wal-Mart TV per visit, and there's no channel surfing. In-store TV advertising is said to be an effective means of swaying undecided shoppers, because three-quarters of buying decisions are made on the spot.

Wal-Mart also operates the largest radio network in the world, which broadcasts four channels of music into all its stores and features special programming, including its Midnight Café program for overnight staff.

Frequent checks of different stores' operations play a significant role in the Wal-Mart philosophy, so the retailer keeps fleets of planes at its U.S. and Canadian headquarters. This way regional managers can make frequent visits to all their stores and keep tabs on what they're selling.

The Supply Chain

Wal-Mart takes advantage of state-of-the-art technology to move merchandise, tracking everything it sells through a vast digital infrastructure:

- Every item is scanned so the system can check which store ordered it before it's given a bar code and placed in the warehouse.
- Every Wal-Mart sale is transmitted via the company's own satellite to the Computer Data Processing Center in Bentonville.
- Shopping and spending patterns are tracked; suppliers are notified when items have been sold and need restocking.
- Suppliers ship new merchandise to regional Wal-Mart distribution centres, each servicing 80 to 120 stores.

- Received in bulk at one end of the distribution centre, goods are automatically broken down into orders for individual stores.
- Each store gets its own trucking bay – "a door per store."
- Full trucks travel to each store several times a day, where merchandise is unloaded and put back on the shelf almost immediately.
- Stores require little storage space and purchased items are replenished within 48 hours.
- Associates have access to this information for every product in the store by pointing a hand-held wireless device at the UPC code.
- Wal-Mart's data system is larger than the Pentagon's.

What Every Supplier Needs To Know

There's a saying in the business world that the only thing worse than being one of Wal-Mart's suppliers is not being one of Wal-Mart's suppliers.

Wal-Mart's reputation for demanding the absolute lowest price of the companies it deals with is so well established that negotiating has essentially disappeared from the process. No vendor these days would dare come to the table with anything other than their best offer.

Dealing with Wal-Mart is, at least, straightforward. There are none of the complex demands many retailers impose on suppliers, such as display fees, damage allowances, late penalties and the like. From the Wal-Mart perspective, such minutiae fall into the category of "inefficiencies."

The result is Wal-Mart's famous one-number negotiation. Ultimately, the pennies shaved off the supplier's price are passed on to the consumer.

Much is expected of vendors beyond the lowest price, however. To avoid becoming what Wal-Mart management labels a "vendor offender," suppliers are prodded to buy time on the in-store TV network, stage special events, or educate Wal-Mart about the ins and outs of the merchandise category they're selling.

The intimacy of this relationship can prove a double-edged sword. Procter & Gamble, for example, taught Wal-Mart everything it knew about the laundry detergent business. It came as a surprise to Procter & Gamble execs when Wal-Mart's own brand of detergent, Sam's American Choice, appeared on store shelves at roughly half the price of P&G's Tide.

Wal-Mart's approach to branding also drew inspiration from the Canada-wide success of Loblaw's President's Choice brand. Wal-Mart was determined to copy and improve upon the Loblaw strategy.

While Wal-Mart claims it will continue to stock other manufacturers' brands, most of the retailer's own forays into proprietary brands have been highly successful. Wal-Mart's Ol' Roy dog food, named for Sam Walton's late English Setter, ousted Nestle's Purina as the top-selling brand worldwide. Weak brands beware.

Wal-Mart's Four Divisions

By 2007 Wal-Mart Stores, Inc. employed more than 1.8 million associates worldwide and over 1.3 million in the United States. The company operated more than 6,700 stores in 14 countries. Each week over 176 million customers shopped one of the following Wal-Mart formats:

Wal-Mart Discount Stores

There are more than 1,100 discount stores in the United States. They average 101,000 square feet in size, employ about 225 associates and offer 120,000 items. The stores' wide, brightly lit aisles with their trademark blue signage are stocked with family apparel, automotive products, health and beauty aids, home furnishings, electronics, hardware, toys, sporting goods, lawn and garden items, pet supplies, jewelry and housewares, among other things.

Wal-Mart Supercenters

The first Super center opened in Washington, Missouri, in 1988. In a little over a decade, Wal-Mart went from having no grocery stores to being America's No. 1 grocer. The Super center is the company's favourite concept: wherever one opens it adds market share, driving general merchandise sales by 30% and up.

There are more than 1,900 Super centers across the U.S., averaging 187,000 square feet. Each employs about 350 associates and offers roughly 142,000 items. Most are open 24 hours. In addition to general merchandise, super centers feature bakery goods, deli foods, frozen foods, meat and dairy products, as well as fresh produce.

Super centers house a number of specialty shops and restaurants such as vision centers, Tire & Lube Expresses, McDonald's, Subway and Radio Grill, portrait studios, hair salons, banks and employment agencies. The stores appeal to wide demographic, drawing a cross-section of customers despite their discount status. By the end of 2006 four Super centers had opened in Canada.

Wal-Mart Neighborhood Markets

Launched in 1998, these smaller-concept stores offer Wal-Mart prices on groceries, general merchandise and pharmaceuticals.

Generally, they're located in markets with Wal-Mart Super centers. The stores average 41,000 square feet in size, employ about 95 associates and stock about 29,000 items. By 2007 there were more than 95 Neighborhood Markets across the U.S. Offerings include fresh produce, deli foods, fresh meat and dairy, health and beauty aids, photo developing, drive-through pharmacies, pet supplies and household chemicals.

Sam's Club

The first Sam's Club opened in Midwest City, Oklahoma, in 1983. A members-only warehouse concept, Sam's Club offers groceries and general merchandise for a membership fee of U.S.$40 for individuals and U.S.$35 for businesses. Ranging from 110,000 to 130,000 square feet in size, the more than 575 Sam's Clubs in the U.S. and six in Canada employ 160 to 175 associates and offer about 5,500 products. The stores' target clientele is small business.

Shoppers can browse items like soft drinks and chips in bulk, upscale merchandise like hot tubs or diamonds, seasonal luxury items ranging from stainless steel barbecues to freestanding electric fireplaces, and a broad selection of seasonal and holiday one-off offerings. Merchandise for both office and personal use includes bulk paper products, furniture, computers and software, groceries, televisions, home furnishings, clothing and jewelry.

Snapshot of the U.S.A?

Observers believe that, taken by itself, Wal-Mart provides the best picture of the state of the American economy. Since the early '90s the company has expanded from its rural roots to become much more representative of the U.S. as a whole. Its offerings have also come to be more broadly representative of American retail.

While dominant in poorer, more rural regions, Wal-Mart remains relatively weak in affluent urban areas. Wal-Mart's Mississippi operations are roughly as big as its New York operations.

And despite its expansion into a broader range of categories and styles of retailing Wal-Mart remains a discounter, so its sales figures can be viewed as a negative indicator. Wal-Mart does especially well when the economy is sputtering.

Competing With Number One

Wal-Mart's strength lies in its command of three aspects of retail: **scale, scope** and **speed**.

In addition to benefiting from its vast size, the retailer can offer a scope of best-selling merchandise greater than a category killer like Toys "R" Us. While Wal-Mart collapses its toy section after the holidays to make room for seasonal merchandise, Toys "R" Us must make do selling toys year-round.

The speed with which Wal-Mart's everyday-low-priced merchandise flies off the shelves is the most mind-boggling part of its winning formula. Turnover is so rapid that conservative industry estimates claim 70 per cent of merchandise has left the store before the retailer has even paid for it.

So what options are left to retailers who want to remain standing in Wal-Mart's wake? Kmart attempted to play Wal-Mart's game in the mid-1990s and ended up bankrupt. Other discounters have managed to thrive in a Wal-Mart-dominated world, however: Costco and Canadian extreme-value retailer Dollarama have cultivated their own style of price slashing, and are doing very well indeed.

CANADA'S GROCERS BATTLE THE SUPERCENTER

Nothing illustrates Wal-Mart's astonishing ability to turn a category on its head than its takeover of the business of selling groceries in America. A decade after opening its first super center, Wal-Mart had become the world's largest grocer.

Canada's food retailers spent 2003 preparing for the arrival of the super center format, well aware of its reputation for driving food retailers across the U.S. out of business.

Wal-Mart entered Canada with the takeover of 122 Woolco stores in 1994, changing the face of retail in the country forever. Sam's Club opened six locations in Ontario in 2003 and 2004, offering fresh food along with a wide range of other merchandise. About a third of the Wal-Mart stores in Canada were already selling some groceries at the time. Then in 2006 the first four super centers opened in Ontario, and Wal-Mart suggested it would soon roll the concept out across the country.

- Both Loblaw Cos. Ltd. and Sobeys Inc. prepared for Wal-Mart's arrival on the Canadian grocery scene by investing in their product mix and buying small competitors.
- Loblaw struck a generous labour agreement with one of its unions.
- Loblaw aggressively promoted its Great Canadian Superstore.
- Superstores offer a full range of groceries, as well as general merchandise, at highly competitive prices.
- Superstore employees are not unionized.
- Prior to the Supercenter's entry into Canada Loblaw, controlled about a third of Canada's grocery sales, under banners including Loblaws, No Frills, Maxi and Fortinos.
- Sobeys replaced some of its IGA locations in Western Canada with Sobey stores, repositioning the chain for greater competitiveness.
- Formats such as Sobeys' Price Chopper and Loblaw's No Frills target price-obsessed shoppers with everyday low pricing, food retailing's main growth area.

What's remarkable is that before even bringing the supercenter north, Wal-Mart managed to transform the Canadian supermarket. Loblaw's mid-decade restructuring and its addition of home décor and fashion product lines partly backfired, however, diluting the President's Choice brand and taking a toll on Loblaw's formerly stellar stock market performance. Nonetheless, broader product assortments and more competitive pricing have proven part of a sea change in food retailing at the start of the 21st century, and Wal-Mart is largely responsible.

The Evolution of Sam's Club

Sam Walton based the Sam's Club concept on Price Club, which opened on the U.S. West Coast in 1979. Taken by itself, Sam's Club would be the 11th-largest chain in the U.S.

When Sam's Club opened in 1983 the focus was squarely on small business. Not everyone could become a member, creating an air of exclusivity. Membership criteria were soon made much looser, as it became clear that to be profitable with its very low margins Sam's Club needed to be accessible to the general public.

To inform the public about the advantages of shopping at a warehouse club with a yearly membership fee, Sam's made use of promotional literature and grand openings that featured entertainment and educational sessions.

Low prices encouraged shoppers to fill their carts with impulse purchases. Sam's first experimented with high-end merchandise by selling full-length mink coats in 1984. The furs had a suggested retail price of up to $8,000, but at $4,500 Sam's Club patrons snapped them up.

In 1993, Costco and Price Club merged. A few months later Sam's Club acquired Pace, reducing the warehouse club sector of the American market to two major players. The mid-90s were marked by dramatically reduced growth and a recognition that the warehouse club market was saturated.

As at Wal-Mart's discount stores, taking efficiency to mind-boggling heights plays a role in Sam's Club's ongoing battle for competitive superiority. Suppliers are asked to contribute to the drive for efficiency by shipping their products on high-quality pallets and packing them in materials that are easy to remove, saving time and money when the goods reach the store.

Sam's also streamlined its communications program, with marketing, merchandising and operations communications going out to all clubs simultaneously to ensure consistency.

SAM'S CANADIAN CHALLENGE

Four Sam's Clubs opened in Greater Toronto in the fall of 2003, and two more opened in London and Guelph, Ontario in 2004. Each store has a floor plate of between 120,000 and 130,000 square feet.

By the time of Sam's Club's arrival in Canada, however, the warehouse club concept was far from new to the country. Price Club, in a joint venture with defunct supermarket Steinberg, opened in Montreal in 1985. Costco subsequently entered in the West, taking over Price Club in 1993 and effectively gaining a monopoly over the warehouse club segment in the Canadian market.

Costco had 61 Canadian stores when Sam's Club first set up shop in Ontario in 2003. (By 2007 Costco had 70 stores in nine Canadian provinces.) The question on many people's minds was whether Canadians would have the appetite for two warehouse clubs.

- This format was a maturing concept in the Canadian market. Sam's lacked first mover advantage.
- With 61 Costco locations in Canada there was relatively little room to expand the warehouse club concept.
- Costco's membership renewal rate was 86% in the U.S. Loyal Costco customers do not typically switch to Sam's.
- Although Sam's Club has more stores in the U.S. than Costco, its performance lags behind Costco on all measures.
- Low food prices help draw consumers to Sam's Club in the U.S. Food prices in Canada are generally lower than in the U.S., diminishing the potential for a competitive advantage.
- Costco is the innovator among warehouse club stores, while Sam's is an imitator. Innovations like selling fresh meat and produce were introduced by Costco and copied by Sam's.
- Canadian chains offer stiff competition in terms of bulk purchase opportunities, a key attraction of warehouse club stores. Loblaw has

its Club Pack program, as well as the highly successful No Name and President's Choice brands.

The Canadian Sam's Clubs are similar in size and in basic merchandising to the U.S. stores, and offer similar amenities. Food typically accounts for roughly 30 per cent of Sam's Club's business, including fresh meats, produce, frozen foods and fresh bakery items. Each store has a "café" with hard benches and plastic laminate tables that will bring back your worst memories of the high school cafeteria.

To turn each Sam's Club visit into a treasure hunt, the clubs aim to refresh the shopping experience by constantly providing new types of merchandise. This approach is well exploited by Costco, which puts luxury items on prominent display in order to capitalize on shoppers' impulses. Both warehouse concepts understand the importance of placing branded merchandise at the store entrance and utilizing end-aisle displays to trigger impulse purchases.

There are several signs that Sam's Club has failed to catch on with Canadian consumers. Several years after its Canadian debut, no Sam's Clubs have opened in the country beyond the original six in Ontario, a clear indication the concept's performance did not meet expectations.

Industry observers have suggested Sam's Club's real role in the Wal-Mart corporate scheme is to prevent Costco from grabbing an even larger portion of the warehouse club market. It may have arrived too late in Canada to achieve this goal.

Toys R… Cheaper at Wal-Mart

During the 2003 holiday season Time magazine ran the headline "Will Wal-Mart Steal Christmas?" The retailer was moving toward dominance of the toy market with a velocity that took category killer Toys "R" Us by surprise. A price war between Wal-Mart and discount competitor Target inflicted irreparable damage on Toys "R" Us, and by 2005 the former market leader had put its stores up for sale.

Once again, Wal-Mart proved itself a killer of category killers. The retailer now handles more than a quarter of the toy sales in the U.S.

The toy store wars of the early years of the decade claimed other casualties. Upscale toy retailer F.A.O. Schwarz filed for bankruptcy twice in 2003 because its formula of selling expensive toys in lavish stores was no match for Wal-Mart's rock-bottom prices. It was left with just two stores when it emerged from bankruptcy, its New York flagship and one in Las Vegas.

Another U.S. toy-store chain, KB Toys Inc., filed for bankruptcy in January 2004, resulting in 4,000 layoffs and 365 store closures. It sold off its Internet business in a restructuring effort designed to help it take on Wal-Mart once more during holiday 2004, and subsequently emerged from bankruptcy. Radical measures were needed to survive in the retail environment the Bentonville Behemoth had created.

Neither KB Toys nor F.A.O. Scharz was able to compete with Wal-Mart's steep price cuts, especially during the holiday sales period. Wal-Mart starts slashing prices in October, pulling in throngs of consumers by offering some items below cost.

In addition, Wal-Mart undercuts its competition by quickly duplicating other retailers' top-selling products using lower-cost manufacturers in China. It leverages its responsive manufacturing and distribution network to get the knockoffs into stores quickly. Competitors' higher-priced versions of the same toys then hold little appeal for consumers.

WAL-MART STYLE?

Wal-Mart is not a name typically associated with fashion, but the retailer's introduction of the George label marked a move from unstylish staples to cheap chic.

Created in 1990 by British designer George Davies, the brand was first rolled out in Wal-Mart's British Asda stores, which it acquired in 1999. George was then introduced successfully to a number of international markets, including Germany, Mexico and Canada. Wal-Mart's embrace of a British fashion label is one sign of how the company has evolved from its small-town American roots into one of the most powerful champions of globalization.

George styles are adapted to the needs of the local market, and the line changes as often as every two weeks to reflect what's selling best. The items on offer cover a much wider spectrum of fashion than Wal-Mart offered previously, including casual wear and suits, leather and cashmere.

Shoppers responded well to the fashions, agreeing they're well made for the price, even genuinely stylish. Moreover, George has been a success worldwide, selling well in both the U.S. and Canada.

Even higher-end fashion retailers like Banana Republic are feeling the pressure to compete. Levi-Strauss, battered by a loss of market share among younger consumers, made a deal to sell jeans at Wal-Mart for under US$30 a pair.

Wal-Mart's success in fashion retailing results partly from having no illusions about sizing. The retailer understands big customers will only be frustrated by a clothing offering that leaves them with limited options.

Working for Wal-Mart

From the senior citizens greeting shoppers at the door to the down-home feel of its advertising, Wal-Mart has traditionally cultivated a friendly, community-oriented image. That image began to crack, however, when employee lawsuits began to pile up in the first few years of the new millennium.

Wal-Mart has come under increasing scrutiny worldwide for its low wages and poor benefits. In the fall of 2003, 245 Wal-Mart contract cleaners in the U.S. were arrested as illegal immigrants, prompting a federal investigation. A group of women employees also filed a discrimination lawsuit against the company, asserting they have been passed over for promotions because of sexist attitudes among Wal-Mart management. Wal-Mart responded by launching a TV ad campaign in the U.S. to shore up its image.

Wal-Mart was also accused of breaking child labour laws. In 2005 the U.S. labour department claimed Wal-Mart stores in several states forced unlicensed teenage workers to use dangerous equipment such as forklifts and power saws. Though Wal-Mart denied the allegations it agreed to pay a fine of US$135,000.

In January 2004 the New York Times ran a story about workers on the late-night shift that were routinely locked in to the store for security reasons. The paper also reported on a Wal-Mart internal audit of one week's time-clock records for about 25,000 employees. The audit found 1,371 instances of minors working too many hours during the day, during school hours or too late at night. It also revealed 60,767 apparent instances of workers missing breaks and 15,705 apparent instances when employees worked through meal times.

Wal-Mart claimed it was implementing processes to ensure associates are paid for their hours and that minors' work schedules comply with the law.

Since then, Wal-Mart's approach to dealing with criticisms has become notably proactive. PR initiatives emphasize the environment and health care, and the retailer argues vocally that its impact on the lives of American families has been overwhelmingly positive.

Wal-Mart's critics, including a number of major unions, have set up websites with names like Wal-Mart Watch and Wake Up Wal-Mart, which track a range of issues relating to the retailer. A typical Wal-Mart Watch headline: "Employees Sue Wal-Mart: Largest Class Action Discrimination Lawsuit in History."

In 2007 Wal-Mart's online Corporate Affairs Message Brief began with the statement that "Wal-Mart is good for America's working families" and ended as follows: "Union leaders should stop attacking a company that serves working families and let people choose for themselves where to shop and work." The website offered Fact Sheets highlighting a range of community and environmental initiatives with titles including "Affordable Health Care," "Disaster Relief," "Charitable Giving" and "Good for America's Communities."

Wal-Mart is now actively addressing the backlash, aggressively defending its corporate practices. Yet while the vast resources at Wal-Mart's disposal position it to influence the attitudes of consumers around the world, the Internet provides an international forum for consumers to publicly air grievances and seek justice. In the Internet Age transparency rules, and PR campaigns have much greater potential to backfire when so many consumers are so well informed.

The Cost of Low Prices

Wal-Mart's famous low prices can partly be credited to the company's treatment of its employees. Anyone contemplating a career at the world's largest retailer anywhere in America should consider the following before filling out an application:

- Wal-Mart does not cover child vaccinations, flu shots or contraception.
- Overall, Wal-Mart spends roughly 30 per cent less on employee health care than its competitors.

- Even when health care is offered, employees often decline to buy it because their wages are so low.
- The average Wal-Mart sales associate earned U.S.$8.25 an hour in 2004.
- At this rate employees make about $14,000 a year. The American poverty line for a family of three is $15,060.

Wal-Mart proponents argue that retail jobs are generally not well paid, and most people working for the company view their positions as temporary. In fact, this is reflected in Wal-Mart's high employee turnover, reported to exceed 44 per cent annually.

Critics worry that Wal-Mart's budget-conscious treatment of its staff could lead to reduced benefits and wages for all retail workers. The customer comes first at Wal-Mart – at the expense of both suppliers and employees.

The Wal-Mart Effect

Even consumers who don't shop at Wal-Mart benefit from its aggressive price policies. By depriving manufacturers of pricing power, the retailer has created an economy-wide Wal-Mart Effect. This, some analysts say, is at least partly responsible for low inflation.

Wal-Mart appears to be better than any other retailer at responding to one of the most cherished values of consumer society: getting the best deal.

For the retailer's critics, the Wal-Mart Effect represents an erosion of diversity in the retail landscape that will result in more poorly paid jobs with negligible health benefits, as traditionally unionized manufacturing jobs vanish from North America. Meanwhile, consumers get used to paying less for products manufactured overseas, often in conditions that would not conform to North American labour and environmental laws.

The Wheel of Retailing

F.W. Woolworth is one of the more than 25 North American chain stores that have closed their doors since 1980. Every generation sees some stores close while new ones take their place, but over the past couple of decades it has become a habit to blame Wal-Mart whenever a retailer goes under.

There are a number of trends that can cause trouble for retailers, and Wal-Mart itself is not immune to them. They include new competition, poor handling of growth by internal corporate operations, dramatic shifts in customer buying behaviour, and organized resistance from unions and government. Wal-Mart has proved adept at minimizing the impact of these forces on its relentless expansion.

The company has been praised for avoiding the cycle known as the "wheel of retailing": A retailer grows big through a successful strategy and builds a substantial shopper base. Then competitors copy its formula, improve upon it and eventually do a better job.

So far Wal-Mart has kept ahead of the competition by aggressively pioneering new sales and distribution practices, and continually offering consumers a wider range of goods at lower prices. No one could criticize Wal-Mart for resting on its laurels, or relying on its size to maintain market dominance.

Just as important, there is still plenty of room for Wal-Mart to grow. It may have conquered rural America, but it has yet to saturate urban markets in states like California and New York, and there is abundant potential for continued international expansion.

In addition, the company is experimenting with taking over anchor stores abandoned by department stores in malls and trying out its small grocery store concept, the Neighborhood Market. Wal-Mart also has its own online music store, which undercuts Apple's phenomenally successful iTunes store by offering songs at 88 cents each, while the iTunes price is 99 cents.

Wal-Mart is also aiming to increase its market share in the following categories:

Pharmacy: By 2005 Wal-Mart was the fourth-largest pharmacy retailer in the U.S., behind Walgreen, CVS and Rite Aid. The retailer enhanced its pharmacy offering by focusing on convenience, putting pharmacy departments near store entrances, adding drive-through pharmacies and rolling out some 24-hour pharmacies. Wal-Mart's pharmacies will continue to grow in popularity among price-sensitive customers who lack the insurance to cover their pharmaceutical purchases.

Consumer Electronics: Wal-Mart is looking at stocking more high-dollar-value products to sustain its growth. Currently second only to

Best Buy in the consumer electronics category, Wal-Mart is poised to become number one as more consumers pick up computers and plasma TVs along with their groceries and pharmaceuticals.

Fashion: Wal-Mart leads the North American apparel market by selling unglamorous items like underwear and socks, but according to analysts the retailer is losing sales of fashion items to competitors like Target, which offers affordable lines from designers such as Isaac Mizrahi and Liz Lange. Fast-fashion emporiums H&M and Zara provide further competition in the cheap-chic market. Although Wal-Mart hoped to woo a hipper clientele with the George fashion line, poor sales of women's apparel in late 2006 suggest fashion-forward consumers remain reluctant to embrace Wal-Mart.

Growing Pains

While Wal-Mart increases its dominance in a growing range of categories, there's no shortage of innovative competitors that are more than capable of holding their own. Dollar stores, in particular, are a convenient alternative for consumers seeking extreme-value goods. They also have the advantage of being small, with relatively short checkout lines, which many Wal-Mart shoppers find appealing. Then there are big-box competitors like Target and Costco, which offer appealing merchandise at low prices.

Wal-Mart faces challenges beyond its domestic market, as well. The sale of Wal-Mart's stores in Germany and South Korea in 2006, and the apparently poor performance of Sam's Club in Canada, suggest that not all of Wal-Mart's plans for international expansion are destined to bear fruit.

Public relations have become increasingly important in countering the negative word-of-mouth resulting from the company's very public legal battles. Since 2005 Wal-Mart has implemented PR initiatives dealing with topics such as the retailer's hurricane relief efforts and the environment, including the building of experimental "green" stores.

Wal-Mart has responded to multiplying political challenges by hiring lobbyists in Washington and boosting donations to political parties. At the federal level Wal-Mart became the No. 1 corporate political contributor in 2006, according to Business Week Online. The Center for Responsive Politics, a non-partisan watchdog, reported that the retailer gave $943,455 in the 2006 election cycle, considerably more than No. 2 contributor General Electric's $788,711. Wal-Mart's growing investment in its political influence represents a dramatic change of philosophy from the avoidance of politics practiced by the company's founder, Sam Walton.

As the U.S. government has declined to get involved in initiatives to boost the minimum wage or improve health-care benefits, the states have become a critical battleground for Wal-Mart. Politicians in at least 20 states have sponsored pieces of legislation – many of them dubbed "Wal-Mart bills" – that aim to force the company to raise wages and offer workers better health benefits. Many U.S. cities have banned large stores like Wal-Mart's super centers, while others have enacted ordinances to force Wal-Mart to pay higher wages.

Clearly the mood of North America's consumers toward Wal-Mart has shifted since the days when it topped Fortune's list of most-admired companies. We may still be living in a Wally Wally World, but factors such as market saturation and new legislation have played a role in decelerating the Bentonville Behemoth's growth, at least in the U.S. Ultimately even Wal-Mart is not impervious to negative word-of-mouth, which the Internet so effectively spreads among consumers the world over.

Chapter 3

The Ministry of First Impressions

Making Contact

YOU form a first impression of a new acquaintance within 10 seconds of meeting, and that impression will determine what you think about him or her for a long time afterward.

Walking into a store for the first time is a lot like meeting someone. Whether they realize it or not, consumers are alert to a whole range of factors when they enter a new store or shopping centre, from the décor to the displays to the friendliness of the staff. People who don't get a good first impression of a store tend not to return.

Beyond the retail environment, anything connected with the brand of a store or a shopping centre can leave a lasting impression. A successful retailer will carefully manage every moment of interaction with the customer. Contact points include all forms of marketing, plus telephone and email communications.

Some retailers become world leaders by communicating their brand through their merchandise, store environment and customer service, without doing much advertising at all. Using all points of contact to make the right impressions on customers adds up to a strong retail brand with high levels of customer loyalty.

TELLING YOUR BRAND'S STORY

Entrepreneurs who attend networking events get used to summing up their businesses in 60 seconds or less. Outlining your company's strengths succinctly to a new contact can be an invaluable tool in promoting your brand. Being able to describe what you do, what your brand provides to your customers and why it matters is just as important for the management of retailers and shopping centres.

A brand can be viewed as the story of a business. Just as stories have always been one of people's primary ways of making sense of the world, brands help unite the people working in a business, and connect the business with the customers it serves. Brand stories propel the stages of the well-known marketing formula: Awareness, Consideration, Trial and Buying.

A strong brand brings together three key elements:

Clarity: What do you want to say? Knowing clearly what the brand stands for determines its content. You must know who you are, what you do, who you do it for, why it matters, and how it differs from what the competition is doing.

Consistency: The brand must communicate the same message at all points of contact and with all customers. When all the store's actions and communications work together in a unified way, the brand reinforces its presence in the marketplace.

Character: Brands with personality are the ones people remember. Giving your brand a little extra flair helps set it apart from the pack, and helps consumers connect with you on an emotional level. When your brand is memorable, people want to buy from you rather than from a competitor with an equivalent offering.

A brand helps you answer fundamental questions about the kind of retailer you are. Why do your customers buy from you? Why does your logo look the way it does? What can you provide shoppers that will make their trip more satisfying? **How can you exceed their expectations?**

Building a strong brand ultimately enables you to make the right impression on customers or potential customers at every point of contact.

Retail through the Customer's Eyes

The in-store experience a retailer creates for a customer is composed of signals: that is, anything that makes an impression. These signals may be rational or emotional, each carrying a message, suggesting something to the customer.

Retail management and staff need to be able to recognize and evaluate these signals. This means experiencing the retail environment like a customer, and taking note of what you're thinking and feeling.

The next step is to accurately identify the aspects of the retail experience that elicit those feelings and thoughts. Knowing what signals your store is transmitting is one of the keys to retail success.

The goal of experiencing your store or shopping centre from the customer's point of view is to build empathy with customers. When there's empathy between a retailer and the people it serves, the retailer is much more likely to anticipate and respond to customers in a consistent manner. Having empathy with your customers reinforces your brand and fosters customer loyalty.

Designing the Experience

Customers consciously and unconsciously tally every signal they encounter as they experience your store or shopping centre. Some signals are positive, some negative and others neutral.

Positive signals promote customer preference, while negative signals cause rejection of your offering. Neutral signals may not push customers away, but they don't draw repeat business, either. Retailers often perceive satisfaction in consumers' response to neutral signals, but in reality these are areas worth targeting for improvement.

Walt Disney was a master at crafting experience signals to make positive impressions on moviegoers and guests at his theme parks. Every element of the experience was carefully sculpted down to the most minute detail, and positioned to promote the intended effect. Disney was clearly asking himself questions like, "What do I want guests to feel and think when they stroll through Disneyland / watch Snow White / buy a hot dog on Main Street?"

Unfortunately, this approach was not successfully exploited at the Disney Store, contributing to its failure to excite shoppers and drive sales.

For retailers and shopping centres, the objective is always the same: eliminate negative signals, overhaul neutral ones to enhance their positive impact, and insert highly differentiated positive signals that build preference.

Carefully designing the customer's experience of your store ensures that every signal throughout her visit is fashioned and placed to register or reinforce a specific impression, and never detract from it. When an experience is unmanaged, it's common for negative signals to cancel out even high-impact positive ones.

MAKING IMPRESSIONS COUNT

Today's most successful retail players have a flair for creating clear expectations of the retail experience they deliver, and then exceeding those expectations. People who walk into Ikea know they'll find contemporary furniture and home décor items at reasonable prices, but they're frequently delighted to discover things priced well below comparable items elsewhere. This is why so few people leave Ikea feeling dissatisfied.

Consumers enter a Home Depot expecting a vast selection of home renovation supplies and tools. They don't necessarily expect an employee to be on hand to custom-trim a new set of blinds on the spot, and they're pleasantly surprised to learn they can return to the store for a workshop on solving storage problems.

Wal-Mart keeps the consumer experience of its stores fresh by dropping prices. Nothing is more pleasing than an item priced lower than it was the last time you bought it. Wal-Mart is also constantly expanding the range of goods it offers.

These three retailers have clear brand identities that are reinforced in all their advertising, and in a range of experiences customers enjoy at the store level. The vast scale of these chains also gives them an advantage in pleasantly surprising customers with broad merchandise selections and, at Ikea and Wal-Mart especially, low prices.

As the following case studies demonstrate, low prices are not always the key to retail success. A retailer can thrive by creating a strong brand that responds to consumer desires in a unique way, creating a satisfying experience for customers at every point of contact.

Reeling 'Em In: Bass Pro Shops

One retailer that has found success by bucking the discounting trend is Bass Pro Shops, headquartered in Springfield, Missouri. The 300,000-square-foot flagship is the state's biggest tourist attraction, with more than four million visitors a year. The largest fishing and hunting emporium in America, it features firing and archery ranges, a four-storey waterfall, a 64,000-gallon aquarium stocked with large-mouth bass, and a taxidermy museum full of stuffed elk, bears and bobcats.

According to the company's PR, "A typical Bass Pro Shops retail store features over 3,500 area antiques and artifacts, up to 400 trophy fish and wildlife mounts and many grand murals depicting scenes reminiscent of the area making it a true destination experience." The Las Vegas Bass Pro Shop even has a live mermaid show.

By creating a one-of-a-kind experience in its stores, Bass Pro thrives without offering merchandise at bargain prices. Though some "experiential retail" concepts have met with a cool reception – the Disney Store and Planet Hollywood are two good examples – the Bass Pro model works because the chain's customers are passionate about their pastimes. Though Bass Pro hardly advertises at all, the average customer travels over two hours to visit one of the stores, and shops for over three hours.

Bass Pro's president, Jim Hagale, directs a team of 60 architects, craftsmen and designers to develop unique environments for stores across the continent. He believes that in-store displays are valuable marketing tools that attract customers, as long as they reflect the local fishing and hunting culture. Before opening an outlet in Destin, Florida, the Bass Pro design team studied local fauna in museums for three months before installing chandeliers adorned with indigenous swordfish and seagulls.

It matters little to loyal customers that many of the items Bass Pro offers are available at Wal-Mart at far lower prices. The retailer makes a point of finding sales associates with exceptionally high levels of expertise, and locates its stores in regions where people will appreciate them. Bass Pro analyzes data on hunting, fishing and boating licences to identify areas where potential customers are concentrated.

Bass Pro's multi-layered approach to creating a memorable customer experience adds value to the merchandise, turning it into more than a mere commodity. Nothing reflects this added value more than the chain's remarkable pricing power.

THE GENIUS OF APPLE

Apple's retail push has dramatically altered both the company's fortunes and the shopping landscape. The stores showcase Apple's beautifully designed and easy-to-use computers and gadgets to their best advantage, and to the delight of growing numbers of Apple fans. The iPod is easily the most exciting piece of consumer electronics launched in more than a decade, and many non-Mac users leave the Apple store with this essential in their shopping bag. In 2007, the much-anticipated introduction of the iPhone reinforced Apple's reputation as the world's leading maker of stylish gadgets – a reputation the company embraced by dropping "Computer" from its name.

Like Bass Pro Shops, Apple's retail success can be partly attributed to the high levels of knowledge of store staff. Apple's computer experts, known as Geniuses, are on hand to answer the questions of the throngs of customers that mob the typical Apple store. People are thrilled to be able to deal with a computer company that will give them friendly expert advice on computer challenges – or even problems with an inexpensive item like an iPod Shuffle – at no cost.

Apple expanded into retailing in 2001, aiming to bring in shoppers and draw a level of attention to Apple computers that they were not getting at traditional computer retailers. The stores keep Apple top-of-mind not only with Mac users, but with people who rely on Windows for their day-to-day computing needs. Merchandise includes the vast array of peripherals and related software available for Macs, dispelling any notion that there are limits to the Apple computing platform. It helps that Apple products are eye-catching, must-have items with high consumer appeal.

The Apple store aims to generate excitement. On weekend nights some have DJs spinning tracks on iPods, and all have free workshops on how to get the most out of Apple products. Some of these workshops have been taught by big-name instructors: director Spike Lee and singer Moby are among Apple's glitterati speakers.

By the end of 2007, Apple was reporting 100 million annual visitors to its stores. The company estimated that roughly two-thirds of these consumers were Windows users drawn by the appeal of the iPod or the iPhone, who could potentially switch to Macs.

Apple makes buying a Mac for the first time a painless task, because employees configure new computers and peripherals for free, before customers leave the store. The Geniuses are skilled people whose job is to answer questions and solve problems, not sell products. The store's approach to customer service was inspired by Ritz-Carlton hotels and their techniques for creating a welcoming environment and putting people at ease.

Apple stores also appeal to the deep-seated wish of modern consumers to belong to a community – another quality they share with Bass Pro Shops and that retailer's community of diehard fishing-and-hunting customers. By using a Mac, or even an iPod, you become part of a group that rejects the homogeneity represented by the Windows world, embracing the creativity and "genius" associated with the Apple brand.

Apple's stores have contributed a great deal to the company's buzz, and the company's long-term strategy to grow market share is paying off. In 2005, Apple's market share was less than four per cent of the U.S. market. Driven partly by what analysts call a halo effect from the iPod and the iPhone, the market share of Apple's personal computers has exploded since then, exceeding 8 per cent by the end of 2007.

A lack of enthusiasm among consumers and businesses about Microsoft's Vista operating system promises to turn more people into Mac users. The fact that an Apple computer remains more expensive than its Windows equivalent, or that iPods and iPhones are more expensive than most competing products, does little to discourage Apple's growing customer base.

From the consumer perspective, the Apple experience means being wowed by the latest in computers and electronics wizardry, and receiving friendly tech help when you need it. Nothing embodies the essence of the Apple brand better than these innovative stores.

JAPANESE INNOVATION: MUJI

The North American debut of Japanese retailer Muji in 2005 was carefully calculated to announce the brand's sophistication to sophisticated consumers: the only place on the continent to buy Muji merchandise was the museum store of the expanded Museum of Modern Art in New York's SoHo. Muji also showcased its stylish and affordable selections at MoMA's West 53rd Street location.

Muji at MoMA offers a pared-down range of the retailer's products to design-savvy shoppers. The store stocks items such as a translucent plastic business card holder for $4.50, an LED flashlight for US$48 and an aluminum coffee table for $180. An ingeniously designed set of cardboard speakers is offered for $42, along with an assortment of office supplies and storage pieces. The style is unadorned and modern, and the Muji brand does not appear on or even inside its products.

Muji followed up its MoMA debut by opening its first U.S. store in Manhattan's SoHo neighbourhood in November 2007. The small store offers about 2,000 of Muji's 7,000 products in 3,200 square feet of retail space, and was intended to test Muji's concept and merchandise selection on the New York City market.

Building on the success of the first two Manhattan locations, the Muji Times Square flagship opened in May 2008. The daylight-filled space on the ground floor of the New York Times Building, a block from Times Square, is the perfect showcase for Muji's sublimely simple aesthetic. The retailer's management waited to find the ideal Manhattan location to wow the city's significant base of international residents. Enclosed by glass walls on three sides, the store's open look and feel help draw visitors into the space. The 4,350-square-foot store offers 1,750 household items and 420 items of apparel.

Muji may be a recent arrival in North America, but it's well-known to international travellers who appreciate a clean, functional aesthetic. Developed as a private brand of Japan's giant Seiyu discount department store in the early 1980s, it was spun off in 1989 to become a Japan-wide retail phenomenon that sells just about every kind of merchandise. The name Muji is an abbreviation of Mujirushi Ryohin, which translates into "no brand, good product."

Muji's back-to-basics philosophy was welcomed by Japanese consumers in the 1980s as an antidote to the brand madness of the country's bubble period.

When Japan's economy cooled in the early 1990s, Muji's unassuming but high-quality products gained an even larger following.

Today the company has more than 320 stores and outlets in Japan, and has expanded beyond the country's borders to Korea, Singapore, Thailand, Hong Kong, Taiwan and China, in addition to establishing itself throughout Western Europe. Its European presence is emphatically urban: all of its eight French stores are in the Paris region, both Spanish stores are in Barcelona, and ten of its sixteen British stores are in London. It follows that Muji got its North American start in the continent's most "urban" city.

In Japan, Muji has no less than half a dozen divisions: Muji Products, which offers household goods such as utensils, cushions, towels and coat hangers; Café & Meal Muji, the chain's bakery cafes and restaurants; a florist selling fresh flowers; the Living Space Planning Division, dealing in building homes according to Muji principles; Muji Campsite, which operates three campsites in Japan; and Idée, the newest Muji brand, which manufactures and sells home furnishings and interior décor items.

As for its retail stores, Westerners would notice similarities to Ikea, but taken as a whole Muji is a concept that has no close parallel in North America. Though the company has been experimenting with slicker marketing tactics this decade, its core philosophy is rooted in the old-fashioned idea of making straightforward products and selling them at affordable prices.

The stores may be utilitarian, but they have a pronounced design aesthetic. Products are presented on plain plywood shelving and unvarnished tables, or in unpainted wicker bins. Items are wrapped in clear cellophane that lets customers see what they're buying. Muji packaging and labels are made from unbleached kraft paper, consistent with the retailer's emphasis on ecological awareness.

Material selection, manufacturing and packaging are all conceived to conserve resources, in addition to keeping prices down for consumers. Like Ikea, Muji's marketing budget is largely devoted to the annual production of a catalogue, which midway through this decade took on a sophisticated, high-design look consistent with the company's current brand direction.

Muji hopes to do what many companies with well-established catalogues have already done, and build substantial online sales. The retailer has invested heavily in its website, targeting to achieve ten per cent of total revenues from online sales.

Will Muji make significant inroads into the competitive North American market? With its distinctive offering and carefully strategized expansion, Muji may well become a sought after brand for urban shoppers across North America in the next decade.

HOME DEPOT TAKES MANHATTAN

One of the most promising areas for the expansion of big-box retailers is urban markets. What happens when Home Depot, the world's leading do-it-yourself store, opens in the world's do-it-for-me capital? Clearly, what Manhattan requires of this suburban big box is a retail concept that resonates with urban dwellers.

As a result, the Home Depot that opened in 2004 on 23rd Street near Fifth Avenue is not your typical building supply outlet. In place of the usual orange metal siding, discreet orange banners announce the Home Depot brand to New Yorkers. Genteel doormen help customers get their purchases into cars and taxis.

The store is different inside, too. Graced by an atrium, it departs from Home Depot's typical one-level layout, allowing shoppers to travel between floors via escalator or elevator.

The offering has similarly been tailored to urban needs. Rather than the usual abundance of lumber and gutter downspouts, the store provides enhanced selections of paint, cabinet hardware, and closet organizing systems. Decor items seldom seen in suburban Home Depot stores, such as oriental rugs, are found here in abundance.

Home Depot carefully analyzed proposed modifications to its concept before entering Manhattan. The retailer conducted extensive studies of local shopping attitudes and dozens of focus groups to determine what New Yorkers wanted.

For one thing, the studies found the city's residents are mostly not do-it-yourselfers. People in the rest of the U.S. may pride themselves on being self-reliant, but New Yorkers are traditionally completely dependent on others when it comes to renovating.

Thus their Home Depot offers a shopping experience tailored specifically to their needs. Unlike a typical suburban store, its centrepiece is a help counter that looks much like the concierge desk of an expensive hotel, where customers overwhelmed by the prospect of doing anything themselves can quickly find guidance and reassurance. The store is pet-friendly, and stocks items seldom seen in other outlets, like a premium "melon chutney" bathroom cleaner.

To help New Yorkers graduate to do-it-yourself from do-it-for-me, the store offers workshops targeted to the local clientele. While people in other places might stop into Home Depot for a drywall workshop, Manhattanites can attend classes with names like "Apartment Plumbing 101" and "Hide Your Television."

To ensure a rewarding shopping experience for NYC customers, Home Depot edited its merchandise selection and created workshops tailored to the unique needs of the market. Through smart research into New York consumer expectations, the retailer created a version of itself that delivers a shopping experience that appeals to its target shoppers. This flexible approach stands Home Depot in good stead as it expands into urban markets that even a decade ago would have been seen as a poor fit for the building supply chain.

Managing Customer Experience

Unlike the four retailers discussed above, many stores and shopping centres still create customer experiences that are not in harmony with the way customers naturally select, purchase and use products or services. Consider the ordeal of purchasing a cell phone: consumers must juggle a bewildering array of technologies, pricing plans, coverage areas, equipment and contracts.

Retailers have the option of managing customer experience to make shopping their stores more rewarding. Experience management needs to be viewed from the customer's perspective, and experience signals must be synchronized with customer desires at each step of the experience.

The four steps customers go through in a typical transaction are:

- Learning about the product or service
- Selecting
- Purchasing
- Using

For retailers and shopping centres, the goal is to ensure a broad range of positive experiences for the customer, creating signals that contribute to a positive impression. This engenders a level of satisfaction that will encourage the consumer to repeat the experience – that is, shop your store or shopping centre again.

Retailers new to experience management often implement improvements in stages, each encompassing a slightly larger portion of the customer's spectrum of experiences.

Comparing two competing businesses reveals the varying degrees to which they manage customer experiences. Consider two hotels: at the first, the experience is distinguished by positive signals like stylish décor, a nice view, the smell of fresh flowers, a cozy robe, a helpful concierge and welcoming assistance. At the next hotel, there's a coffeemaker in the room, and you receive the morning paper free. Obviously, the hotel with the greater number of defined experience signals has a better chance of making the desired impression on customers.

Luxury retailers have traditionally excelled at providing positive signals, but clever discounters are now in on the game. Ikea makes a great impression on its customers with its conspicuous price signs, attractive displays and efficient checkout. The retailer also appeals to people's taste buds with its cafeterias and food sections selling Scandinavian treats. The Ikea experience is so well managed that people happily devote entire afternoons to their Ikea pilgrimages, an international habit that has made Ikea the world's leading furniture retailer.

Every Store's a Stage

Retail space is a stage. Customers care about the physical environments where they select, purchase, and use products and services. Ikea knows this, and this is why you seldom have that big-box feeling when you shop there.

By managing the signals communicated to customers by your store or shopping centre, you can establish a template for the expression of your brand. Customers value experience so highly that even a slight improvement can contribute to building greater customer loyalty.

Beware that entertainment is not the same as a total experience. Attention to the physical aspects of the customer experience is necessary, but not sufficient to establish a lasting preference. A theme store can't reinvent itself every four weeks, so the shopping environment tends to get stale. Consider the harsh economic realities resulting from the overexpansion of both Planet Hollywood and the Rainforest Cafe.

A reality of the retailer-customer relationship is that customers can't always tell you what they want. What's more, the data gathered by traditional customer research techniques is inadequate for designing and measuring total customer experiences. Customers in a focus group can't order up exceptional experiences because they are often unaware of their true desires and feelings, or can't articulate them.

Retailers and shopping centres should ask customers what they think and feel, but also observe their behaviour, and then try to understand why they feel the way they do. Anticipating the customer's needs and desires is the key to delivering a rewarding shopping experience.

Experience vs. Commodity

Shopping attitudes in the current millennium have led to important changes in the consumer value equation. Rather than defining value in terms of price – that is, consistently equating lower price with better value – consumers now often see value in terms of how the quality of merchandise, level of service and store environment relate to the price.

Traditionally, retailers have used a commodity-based strategy that emphasizes price and merchandise assortment. This has resulted in similar offerings and intense price competition. Many retailers have their own house brands and exclusive agreements with suppliers, but these are no guarantee of unique merchandise.

Retailers can escape the traps of the commodity-based strategy by embracing an experience-based strategy. In this way customers receive more value in-store through their shopping experience, in addition to superior products.

Competitors have more difficulty duplicating an experience-based strategy, which can focus on providing superior customer service, stimulating store environments and even superior communities. On the other hand, not giving customers an exceptional in-store experience is like inviting your competition to lure them away.

Respect and the Customer Experience

Respect for the customer must dictate the kind of experience a store aims to deliver. Customers want to be respected in the following ways:

- **Lifestyle.** Today's consumers are diverse. Individual lifestyle differences must be respected.
- **Space.** Give shoppers the distance they need for reflection.
- **Choice.** Consumers want to tailor their retail experience to their own preferences.
- **Time.** Consumers want a fast, efficient shopping experience.

Time is without doubt the most important consideration shaping consumers' reactions to their shopping experiences. Three of the five most highly rated factors across the continent are time-related:

- The amount of time it takes to pay for the purchase.
- The time spent in the store waiting to make the purchase.
- The amount of time needed to pay with a credit/debit card and conduct a smooth transaction.

Arousing Enthusiasm

The consumers of the future will expect more from retailers than just satisfaction. They will expect shopping experiences that exceed their expectations.

- Consumers will want to be repeatedly delighted
- Retailers' most prized customers will act as advocates who spread the word about their shopping experiences
- Consumers can be enthusiastic about the following aspects of the shopping experience:
    - » Fresh merchandise
    - » Attractive store design
    - » Staff with high levels of expertise
    - » Innovative approaches

Customer enthusiasm is key to the best kind of advertising: **Word-of-Mouth**!

What Display Can Do

Display is a key aspect of customer experience. It is consistently exploited by retailers that don't base their competitive advantage on price alone.

Good displays can:

- Create a unique shopping environment
- Show your customers new uses for your merchandise
- Make customers smile
- Sell products and services
- Publicize the store
- Build prestige
- Educate the consumer
- Showcase popular trends
- Invite customers to take a closer look
- Encourage repeat visits

A display should:

- Showcase fresh, exciting merchandise
- Tell shoppers exactly what the store is featuring
- Provide drama, excitement and sales appeal to the product
- Create a positive impression of your store's quality and style
- Highlight one dominant motif
- Reflect the season, and use appropriate colours
- Communicate a clear sales message

The success of Bass Pro Shops illustrates the competitive advantage a retailer can gain by making display a central part of its strategy. The stores may have a theme park atmosphere to people who lack a passion for hunting and fishing, but Bass Pro innovates by displaying merchandise in an environment that evokes the outdoors – where customers will be using their purchases. This generates a level of excitement that gets people's minds off price.

Not every retailer will want to go to Bass Pro's lengths to create an engaging store environment, but more stores could add value by getting creative with their displays.

Better Service, Faster Transactions

Some retailers make customer service one of their primary strengths. Specialty retailers like Apple or Bass Pro attract large numbers of customers without cutting prices because their staff's expertise brings value to the shopping experience. When staff is able to solve customers' problems, customers tend to leave the store happy.

Regrettably, this is often not the case. Stores like the two I just mentioned can set themselves apart from the competition by offering great service because great service is hard to come by. While a luxury clothing retailer might be able to afford to keep the ratio of staff to customers high, we've all shopped our share of stores where we hunt for a sales associate for what seems like hours.

Then there's that other least-favourite experience of the modern consumer: waiting in line. Whether at a supermarket, a fast food restaurant or an airport, no one enjoys hanging around endlessly to complete a transaction. When customers are forced to wait, their level of satisfaction with the shopping experience decreases.

Some retailers have the resources and expertise to provide better experiences by increasing the level of customer service, but retailers paying minimum wage can only expect so much of their overburdened staff.

Additionally, customers increasingly want to define their shopping experiences. Younger consumers in particular are accustomed to accessing the information they want instantly via the Internet.

Touch Screens or the Personal Touch?

Touch screens are one of the technologies transforming the service offering in a growing number of retail categories. They have permanently changed the way we do our banking, and they allow us to pay for gas or print out an airline boarding pass without dealing with an employee. Users of this technology are glad to have the option of serving themselves, especially when it means not waiting in line.

Interestingly, increased automation does not necessarily mean cashiers are being thrown out of work. These employees' job descriptions are changing, and some industries with increased self-service need to hire more staff.

When automating a task genuinely improves the level of service, customers welcome it. When you arrive late for a movie, it's great to be able to get your ticket from a machine instead of waiting in line for a cashier. Self-service kiosks can also be an effective medium for real-time advertising of products and services.

By contrast, the shopping world is littered with kiosks no one uses. These include shopping centre directory kiosks that make locating a store more time-consuming than reading the centre's directory brochure. When a technological advance does not save people time or bring added convenience, it tends to attract few users.

In supermarkets, self-checkout is becoming an increasingly popular way to give hurried consumers a speedy transaction. In addition to self-service at the checkout, some supermarkets are installing kiosks throughout the store to help customers locate items. Some even provide shoppers with handheld scanners that allow them to keep a running tab of their purchases as they shop. Self-checkout has also become a popular option in the building and renovation category, at stores such as Home Depot.

Research has found that touch-screen technology is rapidly becoming consumers' preferred service method. People of all ages are accustomed to using computers to help with a wide range of tasks, and are eager to take advantage of automated services that save time or simplify their lives.

Service Sells

Increasing the automation of some aspects of shopping is in no way incompatible with upping levels of customer service. As Home Depot streamlines the payment process with self-checkout, it is pouring hundreds of millions of dollars into improving sales associates' levels of expertise.

The success achieved by retailers with well-trained employees shows that service sells. Apple discovered that almost a third of the customers that ask for help at its retail stores make a purchase the same day.

Customer Relationship Management (CRM) software and data collected from loyalty programs help retailers become more efficient at managing aspects of customer relations. It's now possible for retailers to "fire" their worst customers – people who abuse return privileges, for instance – while investing more in communicating with the customers who spend the most.

Through analyzing CRM data, mail-order fashion retailer L.L. Bean found its most profitable customers were those buying for the whole household. As a result, the company focused its direct mail efforts on patrons buying across product lines, rather than sending out specialized catalogues for men, women, or kids to people who might not appreciate them. The retailer's customers received 40 per cent fewer mailings, and sales rose by 8 per cent. Customer retention improved, as well.

Successful retailers increasingly look to a variety of forms of new technology to deliver more satisfying customer service. When stores use automation to cut down on the kinds of experiences customers could do without, like waiting in line, they are laying the foundation for more satisfying shopping.

Just as we get a negative first impression of people who talk only about themselves, consumers respond poorly to retailers and shopping centres that don't go out of their way to create experiences that correspond to their desires. Shopping in the 21st century is all about the customer's experience, and the customer knows it.

CHAPTER 4

THE ONLINE CHALLENGE

TECHNOLOGY CHANGES EVERYTHING

TIME magazine's cover of July 20, 1998, bore the threatening headline "Kiss your mall goodbye." The subtitle: "Online shopping is faster, cheaper and better." At the height of the dotcom mania, many North Americans were envisioning the obsolescence of the bricks-and-mortar store as the Internet transformed every facet of day-to-day consumption. Retailers that lacked an online presence pumped exorbitant sums into elaborate websites for fear of being left behind.

We now know it will take more than mouse clicks to kill the shopping centre. Nonetheless, no new development promises to reshape the retail landscape – and society as a whole – as profoundly as the Internet.

By the end of 2006, three-quarters of U.S. households had high-speed broadband Internet access, and half of Americans had come to view the Internet as indispensable to their lives. Of 80 million Internet-enabled U.S. households, three-quarters had purchased products online.

The demographics of the Internet user increasingly reflect the demographics of the population as a whole. The average age of web surfers has risen, while their education level has decreased. The amount spent in the average online transaction is growing.

It is clear the Internet is transforming the way people live in more profound ways than even the dot-com visionaries imagined. Online social networking has swept the planet: MySpace is riding high with over 100 million user accounts, while Facebook has become essential to many people's social lives.

Internet users are sharing thoughts, photos and video clips via 75 million blogs worldwide, and 100,000 new blogs are started each day. Entertainment seekers around the globe log onto YouTube for the latest video novelties, while others construct alternate lives and run imaginary businesses on virtual reality sites like Second Life.

With consumers interacting online in increasingly complex ways, all retail businesses must look closely at the possibilities the Internet provides, including online research, corporate blogging, email marketing, store or shopping centre websites and even virtual stores. As the new century progresses, innovative use of the Internet continues to provide a competitive advantage to companies that embrace forward-thinking approaches to sales and marketing.

THE VERSATILE WEB

Countless dot-com merchants folded during the tech crash at the start of the 21st century, but plenty of e-tailers survived and went on to change the way people shop forever. Amazon transformed the way books are sold, just as eBay created a new framework for selling a wide range of items, from collectables to cars. As the century progresses, however, it's clear businesses have a lot of Internet options at their disposal beyond selling goods online.

The categories that have sold most successfully online have traditionally been "commodities" such as books, software, music or travel - things people don't need to touch or try on before they make a purchase decision. On the other hand, eBay now derives more revenue from selling used cars than from any other category. As consumers have become more comfortable making online purchases the rules for what can be sold on the Internet have changed.

The Internet is now relevant to every retail category. Whether in terms of pricing, merchandise mix, service or marketing, retailers and shopping centres need to keep a close eye on what's happening online and devise new ways of reaching customers via the Web.

Amazon.com has also achieved some of the highest customer satisfaction scores ever seen in the retail industry. Consumers exasperated with poor service, out-of-stocks and other inconveniences at bricks-and-mortar stores often find their online transactions more efficient and rewarding.

Informed Consumers

The Internet's largest impact on retail is the way it provides a range of purchase information to time-pressed consumers. It is now extremely easy for people to educate themselves online, and it is typical for shoppers to arrive at the store armed with more information on a product than the sales associate they deal with.

Store and manufacturer websites and reviews posted on sites such as epinions.com provide plenty of information to help shoppers make informed decisions. It has become the norm to check price and feature comparatives and consumer ratings online before making a purchase.

Because the web is fiercely competitive and price transparency rules, retailers must also be prepared to compete directly with the pricing of competitors across the country, and even abroad. A retailer whose prices are higher than those of online competitors must offer value in other aspects of the transaction. For instance, a shopper may choose an offline retailer over its online competition because the offline store offers a convenient return policy that contributes to the customer's confidence and makes it worthwhile to spend a little more.

Word-of-Mouse

As ever, word-of-mouth is the most effective form of advertising. People are influenced by the opinions of friends, family, co-workers and, most significantly, by complete strangers posting reviews on websites.

Part of the consumer's reliance on the Internet for information about products and services results from the lack of information in modern advertising. At one time it was typical for ads to communicate a product's features and benefits. With marketers' more recent focus on building an emotional connection with the consumer and trying to make their ads stand out in an ad-cluttered world, consumers have started to feel manipulated. Many no longer expect advertising to provide reliable information. As a result, they turn to other consumers, both people they know and strangers online, to provide the information they need to make purchases that suit their needs.

Retailers and shopping centres that fail to deliver good products, good service or enjoyable shopping experiences do so at the risk of having negative word-of-mouth – now word-of-mouse – spread around the world.

The new ease with which people can share their grievances with thousands of other consumers online means retailers and shopping centres need to place new emphasis on providing friendly, responsive customer service to help smooth over complaints. Customers must be encouraged to share their complaints with management before they relate bad experiences to others. Otherwise, angry or dissatisfied consumers may write negative Internet reviews, which have the potential to sway the opinions of existing and potential customers.

SOCIALIZING AND ENTERTAINMENT

Chatting, online personals and cyberspace communities built around common interests revolutionized the way people interacted by the end of the '90s. But no one foresaw the phenomenal success of social networking sites like MySpace, which had more than 150 million user accounts by the beginning of 2007.

By providing a framework for people to post photos and music, write blogs, share personal information and build vast networks of online friends, MySpace quickly became an obsession for many Internet users. After Rupert Murdoch's News Corp. paid US$580 million to acquire MySpace in 2005 the site's popularity continued to grow, and it soon surpassed Yahoo! as the most visited website in the U.S.

At the same time the popularity of other social networking sites was on the upswing. Most focused on a particular type of consumer: LinkedIn targeted professionals, while Facebook catered to college students. Social networking went mobile in 2006 when MySpace and Facebook became accessible via cell phone.

Meanwhile people were looking more and more to the Web for entertainment. Launched in early 2005 and snapped up by Google for US$1.65 billion in 2006, YouTube allowed people to view a variety of forms of video entertainment, including user-generated content – that is, homemade video. The site soon accounted for 60% of all videos watched online.

With 100 million downloads per day and 20 million unique users per month YouTube accounted for almost a third of U.S. online multimedia entertainment by the end of 2006, transforming the way people consume video. The site's rise to popularity was not without its snags, however. Viacom Inc., the owner of cable networks including MTV, VH1 and Comedy Central, filed a

US$1 billion copyright lawsuit against the video-sharing site and its corporate owner, Google Inc., in 2007.

The inadequacy of old copyright laws in face of Internet technology will continue to present challenges for the creators and broadcasters of arts and entertainment. Many forms of culture now enjoy their greatest popularity as Internet content.

The Honda Element's MySpace Page

While there is no easy recipe for employing social networking sites as effective marketing vehicles their potential usefulness to marketers is clear. Honda, for example, created a MySpace page to promote its Honda Element compact crossover SUV. The page invites MySpace users to enter a contest to create computer desktop wallpaper, and thumbnails of the finalists' wallpapers are posted on the page.

This multi-layered marketing initiative encourages MySpacers to develop a sense of ownership in Honda's marketing campaign by creating content – the wallpaper – and by participating in picking a winner. At the same time, Element enthusiasts have the opportunity to connect with others who share their fascination in this "cool" Honda offering and build a sense of community around it.

There is also a link from the MySpace page to the Element Friends microsite, which offers a number of fun online activities targeted to young adults. The net result is that Element lovers become more invested in the marketing campaign with every click of the mouse, and the longer they spend on this network of websites the more likely they are to want to own one.

The success of MySpace, Facebook and YouTube shows that what people enjoy most in an online experience is the opportunity to socialize, interact, be entertained and have fun. As a result retail and shopping centre websites and marketing campaigns should also aim to build communities and provide a social experience. When this is done effectively consumers become enthusiastic about the offering and value the brand more highly than before.

The Generation Gap

According to Nielsen/Netratings, kids aged 2 to 11 spent an average of six hours and 39 minutes online in September 2003. By September 2006 that average had increased 41 per cent to almost 9 hours and 24 minutes.

The time teens spend online increased 27 per cent over the same period, from an average of 21 hours and 4 minutes in 2003 to 26 hours and 48 minutes in 2006.

- Young adults ages 13 to 24 spend more time on the Web than with any other media source.
- Older adults are more attuned to traditional media such as TV, radio and newspapers.
- According to a 2006 BIGresearch study, 70% of young adults 18-35 regularly use a cell phone, 38% use instant messaging regularly and almost 33% use an MP3 player.
- Younger consumers are adept at avoiding traditional advertising: nearly 23% use Digital Video Recording, enabling them to watch broadcast content without commercials.

Internet Personals

Another vast area of Internet trade revolves around romance. The posting of online personal ads, or "profiles," has become so widespread that it has permanently revolutionized the way people hook up.

The biggest Internet dating sites include eHarmony.com, Matchmaker.com and LavaLife. In 2007, leader Match.com claimed profiles on its site were viewed an average of 5 million times per day, and that the site had more than 15 million members, either with profiles posted or who actively used the site. Leading sites also provide users with wireless dating and communications opportunities via cell phone.

Demographics help explain the popularity of Internet dating: singles 18 and over now make up 40% of the population. In addition, one-third of people who use online dating services are married, according to Marketdata Enterprises.

Yahoo! personals introduced recommendation engines to online dating.

Made popular by Amazon.com, recommendation engines provide recommendations based on similarities in consumption patterns between consumers, matching people who are interested in both Mozart and skydiving, for instance.

Brief "face-to-face" encounters, dubbed speed-dating, have also enjoyed growing popularity. Speed dating is offered by services such as Speedmatching.com, 8minuteDating and the UK's Speedflirt.

Blogging

Anyone who wants to share their thoughts with the world can now publish them online in a blog. Billionaire Mark Cuban, for example, writes a blog about his basketball team, the Dallas Mavericks, and about technology. Talk-show host Rosie O'Donnell uses her blog to talk about her kids, post poetry, and talk about a range of topics she feels strongly about.

Blogs – a contraction of "Web logs" – have become the fastest-growing form of online publishing. Many people post blogs on their MySpace or Facebook pages, while a number of sites featuring more advanced blogging software make it easy for anyone to have a blog. The most popular include TypePad, LiveJournal, Wordpress.com and Vox, which offers the added benefit of allowing you to control who sees your blog.

"Mo-blogging" or "moblog" is on-the-scene reporting from bloggers armed with cell phones or other portable devices. Many bloggers post photos, video and text to their blogs from wherever they happen to be.

Blogging software allows bloggers to configure the appearance of their blog by choosing themes, background images and layout styles. Additional features known as "widgets" can be added to blogs, including lists of the most-read and most commented-on posts, music players, video clips and "feeds" from selected Web services.

Blogs also play a role in enhancing the transparency of corporations and institutions that consumers increasingly demand. Corporate blogs can help communicate new initiatives and initiate productive discussions both within a company and externally. An externally available blog appearing under the name of a politician or CEO can lend an organization a level of credibility that can never be achieved through one-to-many marketing means such as the website. Of course, interactive blogs are also a two-way street, and can be used by consumers against companies that break their promises.

In Debt and Online

One of the changes the Internet brought to human interactions with the first wave of personal websites in the '90s was the ability to share personal information – including live video of an individual's daily household activities – with Internet users around the world. Blogging under an alias is now a popular means to publicize details of one's life that might be too personal or awkward to share with friends or relatives.

Notably, there has been an explosion in blogs devoted to consumer debt. Sites with names like "We're in Debt," the "No Credit Needed Blog" and "Make Love, Not Debt" have proliferated as overspending consumers have gone public with their debt challenges and search for solutions. Bloggers on these sites typically post their total debt or net worth – typically in the negative figures – and describe their daily expenditures.

Some of these bloggers are attempting to battle the challenge of credit card debt by publishing detailed accounts of their spending and inviting input on how to reduce debt and spend less. Sites like No Credit Needed help provide solutions, such as reducing or eliminating the use of credit cards. Not only do consumers use the Internet to exchange tips on where to shop, they use the medium to help each other not shop.

Online Marketing

For marketers the Internet offers an astonishing range of possibilities combined with ever-growing reach. In the future few successful advertising campaigns will be without a fully integrated Web component. Both the Web and e-mail present exceptional potential for targeting both business-to-business and consumer markets.

The interactivity of the Internet has changed the way marketers communicate with consumers, and has given consumers ways of communicating with marketers that never previously existed. The Internet has a significant advantage in terms of immediacy: it is able to deliver messages that are directly relevant to the current interests and recently displayed actions of the customer.

The ability of the customer to provide marketers with detailed information on how she wants to be marketed to provides marketers with the necessary tools to make ads that appeal to the consumer. If the ad a consumer sees on her cell phone, laptop, iPod or other device is tailored to her interests she will be much more receptive to the message. Ads that are not highly relevant will increasingly be ignored.

As ad-avoiding technologies continue to proliferate, the most effective advertising will be the message targeted precisely to a receptive user.

In the future, all effective advertising will be TARGETED and RELEVANT.

Completing the AIDA Cycle

Traditionally, marketing has only been able to address one or two stages of the Awareness – Interest – Desire – Action (AIDA) cycle. Advertising, for instance, can lead a customer to act but cannot complete the transaction. The Internet, on the other hand, allows the customer to move through initial awareness to purchase.

Learning through Internet Marketing

The expensive direct marketing methods of direct mail, telesales and direct sales can easily serve as a basis for quantitative marketing learning. The Internet, on the other hand, can capture site navigation information, information retrieval and purchase behaviour, and user-supplied profile and preference information, all at a much lower cost.

Email also provides for an accessible recollection of interactions: an emailed customer complaint about a defective product may more easily be picked up than a customer conversation with a sales associate.

Putting Control in the Customer's Hands

Marketers must abandon marketing "to" consumers and instead market "with" them. This means seeking the customer's permission to commence and continue an ongoing dialogue. This option exists in direct sales and telesales, but the Internet enables the permission decision to be made more conveniently and at lower cost to the vendor.

Just as the Internet provides ample opportunity for the marketer to be responsive during a customer transaction, it allows the customer to maintain a new level of control over the experience. In the online environment the possibility of customer defection to a competitor's site is ever-present. As a result, marketing communications must be designed for access that can be easily controlled by the customer.

A customer who cannot find all the answers she seeks on a website quickly and easily can defect to the competition's site in a couple of clicks. Thus websites must be adapted to provide consumers the information they desire, and supply multiple paths to obtaining it.

SPAMNESIA

Email is potentially one of the most useful elements of an Internet marketing campaign for retailers and shopping centres. If put to good use, an email campaign can forge a valuable link between a store or shopping centre and its customers, cultivating loyalty and providing people with information that will help them become more satisfied shoppers.

In a world of overflowing inboxes managing a successful e-mail marketing campaign can be a formidable challenge. It's not easy for email marketers is to make their communications stand out.

Meanwhile spam barriers deflect many legitimate emails, and spammers continue to hone their techniques.

Despite the irritation of spam, people continue to register to receive permission-based e-mail. More than three-quarters of Canadian Internet users have registered for permission-based e-mail on at least one website, and more than half say they are willing to provide their e-mail address to retailers and other companies when requested.

Fear of receiving spam is the most commonly cited reason for refusing to provide an e-mail address. Two-thirds of Canadian Internet users say they do not wish to receive unsolicited e-mail under any circumstances.

The message for marketers is that once they have subscribers' permission to include them on an email list they must hold their interest by providing relevant and intriguing content. By inviting customers to fill out a profile page and giving them options in terms of the information they receive, marketers can help ensure they communicate neither too much nor too little to their customers.

The key is to make the information provided in marketing emails clearly relevant to each person that receives it. Failing to strike the right balance will contribute to losing the customer as an email subscriber.

BUILDING STRONG EMAIL RELATIONSHIPS

- Obtain affirmative consent from customers and build files responsibly. Email campaigns must be permission-based.
- Confirm email registrations by sending customers a confirmation email immediately upon sign-up.
- Survey customers or have them complete a profile page to find out what kind of information they'd like to receive.
- Custom-tailor email marketing messages based on customer interests and preferences.
- Send customers only valuable, relevant offers.
- Respect consumer privacy. Email addresses and personal information must not be shared or sold without the express consent of the consumer.
- Post links to your privacy policy where they are clearly visible on both email messages and websites.
- Carefully manage the amount of information you send customers – avoid over-communicating.
- Provide an easy one-click opt-out system in all emails and on the website.
- Provide full customer assistance and promptly answer email messages.
- Maintain an up-to-date, responsive database and remove those who haven't responded over an extended period.

INTERNET SURVEYS

The Internet has revolutionized many aspects of market research, and the online survey in particular has provided marketers with a versatile, cost-efficient tool to gauge consumer attitudes. Data can be gathered quickly, conveniently and affordably using online surveys, which quickly proved a valuable alternative to traditional mail and phone surveys.

Online surveys are a reliable source of data now that Internet use is nearly universal in developed countries and a number of companies – SurveyMonkey being arguably the most successful – have introduced online survey methodology that can easily be custom-tailored to the needs of a business or organization.

Making use of Internet surveys throughout the year to gather up-to-date information on customers provides an exceptionally useful source of insight into customer behaviours, attitudes and needs. Making online surveys a key component of your marketing research has the potential to profoundly impact on your ability to understand your customers, respond to their desires and ultimately exceed their expectations.

Those implementing an Internet survey program have several options to choose from in terms of reaching respondents and collecting their answers. Each method has its pros and cons.

Email surveys are questionnaires involving the use of email, and are easily implemented when targeted at small numbers of people. Repeat questioning is facilitated, and they are effective for collecting free opinions.

Web surveys can incorporate multiple choice, free response and other formats. Real-time tabulation is possible.

Electronic meeting rooms are discussion surveys using online meeting or chat rooms and mailing lists. A coordinator who has skills in providing the topic and generating enthusiasm is required. Although skilful control can result in a wealth of information, analysis is difficult.

RESPONDENT SELECTION

The characteristics of the sample completing an online survey are partly determined by the method used to obtain their cooperation.

Public invitation method: Respondents are recruited through a website link, a contest or via banner ads on search engines. This approach is not appropriate for ordinary surveys, due to the inability to select respondents' circumstances.

Semi-public invitation method: Respondents are recruited by contracting survey notification to a company that has an email address list.

Registered panel method: Potential respondents are registered as members of a panel, and respondents for each survey are selected from among panel members according to their individual circumstances. Using this method it is possible to conduct a survey only among respondents who meet required conditions.

Advantages of Online Surveys

The greatest strength of Internet survey data collection is the potential to collect a large amount of data in a relatively short amount of time. Hundreds of respondents can fill out a survey within a matter of days, and all of these responses can be automatically inserted into a database. In addition to its efficiency, web-based data collection can be remarkably flexible, allowing randomization of question order and complicated skip patterns.

When compared to traditional survey techniques using mail, telephone and customer intercepts, Internet surveys allow for extremely fast turnaround. In order to interview 2,000 people, a typical telephone survey may require over 80,000 telephone calls and two months to complete, while an Internet survey can be broadcast to hundreds of people in a matter of minutes. An entire web survey project can be completed in a couple of days, where printing alone can take a week for a mail survey.

Most web-based surveys are announced with an email message that contains a link to the survey page. This format allows users to respond at their convenience and removes many of the barriers in responding to either mail or phone surveys. This results in significantly higher response rates.

Traditionally low, mail response rates hover in the 2%-3% range. Telephone surveys allow for retries when the contact isn't available; consequently, they can yield results at the 10% level. Comparatively speaking, in-person shopping centre intercept surveys have high response rates – between 20% and 40% in our experience, depending on the centre and the approach taken by the survey team. These favourable response rates underline the continuing relevance and effectiveness of traditional shopping centre intercept surveys, even as Internet survey methodology is adopted by an increasing number of businesses.

DISADVANTAGES: SAMPLE QUALITY

The most questionable aspect of web-based survey methodology is whether a representative sample of consumers will have the opportunity to respond. Volunteer respondents to online surveys may not represent the target audience for a given product, store or shopping centre.

Challenges arising from the self-selection of respondents can be countered by qualifying respondents carefully, ensuring that they are in fact potential or existing customers before allowing them to participate in the survey.

TECHNICAL PROBLEMS

When considering the use of Internet surveys to gather information on customers, marketers need to be aware of a variety of technical glitches that can occur as respondents fill out surveys.

Freezes/crashes: The respondent may be unable to complete the survey due to a browser freeze or server crash, resulting in missing data. To minimize this risk, try to keep the survey relatively short. If you have a long survey, you may want to split it across several pages. A respondent's answers are submitted at the end of each page; then if the respondent is disconnected on the fourth page of the survey, you have already safely captured the first three pages of data.

Error messages: A programming glitch in a survey can result in a confusing error message as a respondent fills out the questionnaire. To avoid this problem, surveys must be tested and re-tested rigorously to ensure all the "bugs" have been worked out. Attractive and helpful error messages can help mitigate any challenges a respondent might experience while completing an online survey. For example, if a respondent accidentally skips a question, a customized message can instruct the respondent to return to the question and complete it.

Double entry: In many surveys, it is possible for the same subject to return to the survey and complete the questionnaire several times. The best way to avoid this problem is to recruit a specific sample of respondents, assign each respondent a unique ID, and allow each ID to be used only once. Using the respondent's e-mail address to assign a unique ID is not a foolproof method, as many people have several e-mail addresses.

Beyond Segmentation

Just as the Internet has changed the way we shop, it has led to a shift in the way we think of consumer behaviour. In the online world, consumers are not always the people their demographic profiles suggest they are.

Think about the way you watch TV: sometimes you channel surf, while at other times a show will hold your interest for an hour or more. People shop the same way, sometimes looking for a specific item and sometimes taking their time to browse. These differing patterns have been described as occasions.

Segmentation has traditionally relied on the formula that who consumers are dictates how to market to them. Marketers have come to rely on demographics because they need analytical criteria – quantifiable data that indicate shoppers' attitudes and habits – and not because shopping behaviours and demographics are intrinsically linked. On average and over time characteristics such as age, gender and wealth correlate with shoppers' attitudes and habits, such as credit card usage, and are thought to be the best indicators of typical future behaviours.

The increasing sophistication with which advertisers are approaching their online activities is a direct result of research into the varied ways that people use the Web. As marketers gain a more complete understanding of consumers' online habits they become better armed to market to them in ways consumers feel more inclined to welcome.

Here are some of the key factors shaping the online marketing environment as we move into the second half of the decade:

- More than four in five U.S. marketers cite building brand awareness as an online advertising objective.
- More than two-thirds of U.S. marketers cite new leads and customers as objectives in online advertising, while half say they want to drive sales.

- Advances in online creative permit Internet campaigns that are highly interactive and provide prompt responses.
- Retailers, consumer packaged goods and pharmaceuticals have found success connecting with customers through online direct response programs.
- Coupons can be used as a "hook" to begin the value exchange, after which customers are communicated with directly.

WHY SHOP ONLINE?

Consumers would not be enthusiastic about shopping online if it didn't deliver concrete benefits. The fact is, prices online are often lower than they are offline. E-tailers are able to offer better deals because the Internet lowers transaction costs, cutting out middlemen and resulting in lower prices for the consumer.

The convenience of shopping from home is another selling point. What this means is that traditional stores are in some cases becoming showrooms. Sony and Apple stores are designed to show off merchandise, in the expectation that many customers will make their purchases online.

Sophisticated retailers take full advantage of multi-channel selling, which can involve a website, a phone-in order service, a catalogue and even a TV home-shopping channel in addition to traditional stores. Retailers that make innovative use of selling channels appeal to consumers' desire for convenience and enhance their competitiveness as compared to stores that focus exclusively on their bricks-and-mortar operations. In addition, online sales can be leveraged to clear out items without taking up costly retail space, and provide an inexpensive way to test new products and retail concepts.

Many "integrated retailers" have made good use of the medium to expand their business. These retailers sell merchandise online while using their websites to drive traffic to their physical stores. Best Buy, Home Depot and Nordstrom are a few good examples.

Meanwhile, merchants that operate exclusively online continue to make headlines through exponential growth and by continually finding new ways to revolutionize the way business of all sorts is conducted.

Amazon.com

From its beginnings selling books, Amazon has branched out into offering a variety of items – DVDs, software, apparel, jewellery, furniture – reinforcing its position as a global retailer to be reckoned with. Amazon's chief executive, Jeff Bezos, claims the site can sell pretty well anything apart from cheap, bulky items like garden rakes.

Launched in 1995, Amazon.com zoomed from $16 million in sales to $1.6 billion in just four years, a feat unequalled by any retailer. Net sales had increased to $10.71 billion in 2006, up 26% from the previous year.

Amazon.com's business model is built around five fundamentals that are not expected to change: low prices, a big selection, availability, convenience, and good information about products.

Amazon also employs a recommendation engine that allows Amazon's visitors to create personalized shopping profiles. This is one of the best examples of active retailing on the Web: the recommendation engine effectively takes merchandise to the shopper, rather than expecting the shopper to search and find other merchandise by herself.

While Amazon benefits greatly from being one of the earliest established and best-known brands online, e-tailers and established retailers are making use of this same model to move goods in an ever-expanding range of categories.

eBay

Like Amazon, eBay started in 1995, and has since become a powerful force in every marketplace, mediating sales ranging from baseball memorabilia to nuclear power plants. In 2006 eBay generated consolidated net revenues of $6.0 billion, a 31% increase over 2005.

The online collectable market is still synonymous with eBay: over 100 Barbie dolls are sold on eBay every hour. However, the Internet's largest auction-style marketplace for buying and selling cars and trucks is eBay Motors, and autos have become eBay's most lucrative category.

The site may have started out as an online auctioneer, but it now hosts websites for tens of thousands of stores. Clothing and accessories bought through eBay account for more than US$1 billion in annual sales.

While the threat of fraud is the single most significant factor preventing eBay's popularity from shooting even higher into the stratosphere, the auction site has millions of satisfied customers – not to mention hundreds of thousands of sellers making a living partly or exclusively through the site.

In addition to its Internet marketplaces, eBay generates revenue through a growing assortment of websites and online services:

- PayPal, eBay's online payment service, was founded in 1998 and acquired by eBay in 2002. PayPal now has tens of millions of user accounts.
- Skype is a communications network that allows users to communicate over the Internet using both voice and video.
- Shopping.com is a leading shopping comparison site that features consumer reviews from epinions.com alongside reviews from the experts.
- Rent.com is the most popular rental accommodations hub in the U.S.
- eBay also owns Kijiji, Gumtree.com and several other online classified ad sites around the world, in addition to a minority stake in the popular craigslist.org.
- StubHub is an online marketplace for the resale of events tickets.

Like Amazon, eBay has leveraged its first-mover advantage to become a formidable force in online commerce. Industry observers following the latest in online retail need to keep a close watch on the growing range of activities of these Internet giants.

THE IMPACT OF E-COMMERCE

Travel agents were forced to rework their business model thanks to the online travel boom, and music stores must contend with the availability of CDs on sites such as Amazon, not to mention the popularity of downloading MP3s. Canada's largest book chain, Indigo Books & Music Inc., was forced to reinvent itself as a "cultural department store," decreasing books as a part of its inventory and selling more gifts instead because of Amazon's success. And need we mention that online porn sales have become a multi-million dollar business?

While offline retailing is not about to disappear, it behooves all retailers to keep an eye on developments online, in addition to ensuring their own web presence is working to their best advantage. Keeping ahead of competitors' use of the Internet is crucial to thriving in 21st-century retail.

Retail Websites

Successful retailers know the value of an attractive storefront, and even in an age of big-box utilitarianism an eye-catching window display can be a valuable sales tool. The virtual storefront, the website, is arguably even more important in terms of making a good first impression on customers, and retailers that neglect their site do so at their peril. Even stores that do no selling online need to ensure their website is both useful and an accurate reflection of their corporate identity. A hard-to-use website suggests the company does not have the customer's best interests at heart.

The retail website can be used to advertise and promote, improve recruitment, enhance marketing positioning and, of course, to sell merchandise. Above all, the website is all-important as a representation of a company's products, services and brand. An underperforming site will send shoppers elsewhere, since competitors are never more than a click or two away.

Retailers are taking advantage of the web's potential as a marketing medium in a variety of ways. Making sure your website comes out at the top of a Google search has become a prime marketing objective for many companies. Paying for sponsored links on search engines is also said to give an excellent return on investment. Retailers that are prepared to compete aggressively on price can make use of sites such as eBay, Yahoo! and Amazon as trading platforms for their goods.

The Microsite

Another cost-effective use of the Web employed by a range of consumer-oriented companies is the microsite. A microsite is a mini-website separate from a company's main website, with its own URL. The microsite can deliver focused, relevant content about a specific product, service or campaign, and can easily be optimized in search engine rankings.

Microsites have enjoyed increasing popularity because they help build community around the site's focus, and can encourage word-of-mouth and pass along, also known as viral marketing. They make a great deal of economic sense as the market for advertising moves online. As traditional media become less effective, online communities and the peer-to-peer sales approach become increasingly relevant.

Unilever's Dove brand, for instance, capitalized on its enormously successful Campaign for Real Beauty by launching campaignforrealbeauty.com, a site that allows customers to watch the latest ads and join in the discussion on the popular and timely campaign. The site prominently features a tell-a-friend link, which makes it easy for enthusiastic customers to promote Dove products to others.

VIRTUAL RETAIL

Distinct from online stores or e-commerce websites, virtual stores are enjoying increasing popularity among businesses as a means of encouraging interest in their brands among virtual reality devotees. Companies including Nike, Amazon, American Apparel and Telus have set up stores on the virtual reality site Second Life, which boasted over 4 million residents by the beginning of 2007.

While many Second Life users have taken advantage of the complex social and economic networks created on the vast site to build virtual businesses – which some see as a useful dry run to launching a similar business in the real world – established companies set up shop on the site to promote themselves among its enthusiastic users.

The virtual stores are built on virtual real estate and represented through computer-generated images of the store's exterior, interior and displays, which feature the company's branding prominently and allow visitors to browse assortments of virtual merchandise. Consumers who become fans of a brand in their virtual lives have the option of logging onto the company's e-commerce website – or even walking into a real-life store – to purchase the goods they've experienced in the virtual world.

Both microsites and virtual stores leverage the Internet's potential as a marketing medium more inventively than older (and relatively ineffective) forms of Web advertising such as banner ads and pop-ups.

As the popularity of social networking sites like MySpace has made clear, one of the online activities people are most drawn to is socializing. Innovative marketers can build enthusiasm for a store, product or service by creating a unique online presence and making it easy for people to share information about it via word-of-mouse, thus building community. This one-to-one communication will increasingly replace the mass media one-to-many model.

The Ideal Shopping Centre Website

As e-commerce is never one of the main functions of a shopping centre website, a centre's site has a very different role to play than a retailer's site. While integrated retailers sell some merchandise online, shopping centre sites are largely e-commerce free – except perhaps for gift card sales. The shopping centre site's primary goal is always to drive traffic to the centre.

A shopping centre website can drive offline traffic in a number of ways. Most importantly it can help people find centre retailers by providing an interactive store directory with a number of search options, so customers can locate a store through store name, category and keyword searches. The site can encourage customers to come to the centre by providing information on sales, promotions, events and new stores. Job seekers are among the most avid users of shopping centre sites, and their job search should be made easier through a careers page that is attractive and detailed.

The shopping centre website can also build the centre's database of email addresses by encouraging customers to register for e-bulletins and contests. As gift cards are an important revenue source it should promote centre gift cards. And every page of the site should favourably reflect the shopping experience the centre offers and build the centre's brand.

A shopping centre website needs work if:

- The store directory is not easy to use
- Centre gift cards are not promoted
- Job search data is minimal or hard to find

Every shopping centre site must provide basic information that enables time-pressed consumers to enjoy a productive shopping trip to the centre, and must do so in a way consistent with the centre's branding and advertising.

The sites of shopping destinations in the portfolio of Taubman Centers Inc., one of the world's leading shopping centre management companies, feature a section called My Mall. This part of the site encourages customers to build their relationship with the centre and make shopping trips more productive through features including My Favourite Stores, My Shopping Trips and My Gift Reminders. As customers invest time in using these functions to organize their shopping activities they are apt to become more loyal to the centre.

A shopping centre website should aim to effectively communicate the centre's strengths and make it easy for customers to plan their shopping mission. That way, customers will get the most out of the time they spend on the website, and at the centre. A website that excites and empowers customers will be all the more effective in inspiring them to visit the centre.

New Possibilities

Where businesses can use the Internet to enhance their marketing and operations they will increasingly leverage its power to grow revenues and market share. The Internet permits businesses to become more competitive by cutting out middlemen and reducing their staff and overhead, as marketers engage consumers in a dialogue that can help develop communities around products, stores and shopping centres.

A retailer that doesn't sell online still needs to make innovative use of its website to drive traffic and reinforce its brand. It must also use email, blogs and perhaps microsites to communicate with customers and encourage them to promote an offering to each other. Offline retailers that exploit niches where online retailers cannot satisfy consumers can thrive in a world where virtually everyone does some shopping online.

The Internet has become indispensable to day-to-day life. Responding to the Online Challenge means rethinking our communications models and using new technologies to reach consumers who are more informed than ever.

CHAPTER 5

KIDOPOLY

GROWING UP ENTITLED

CHILDREN have never had so much money and power at their disposal, and have never wielded so much influence over their families' purchasing decisions. Kids' desire for products they use only indirectly is increasingly driving market trends, while some analysts suggest household decision making has been ceded to kids.

Kids' power over their parents extends to a range of items including far more than the breakfast cereals, snacks and toys that advertisers focused on a generation ago. These days, North American kids are said to influence over US$500 billion of their parents' spending a year on a diverse range of items including vacations, electronics, appliances and cars.

Research indicates kids' enthusiasm for the Internet largely accounts for this trend. In the Information Age, wired youth wield more power in the household than children in pre-Internet times. Kids use a portion of the hours they spend online to dig deep for facts about potential family purchases. Guilt-ridden Boomer and Gen-X parents are much more likely to listen to them than the parents of previous generations, too.

In addition to their burgeoning influence, kids also enjoy increased spending power. Kids in North America are said to account for over US$20 billion in direct spending annually. Because kids have become such a significant spending force, marketers are trying to reach them in a variety of inventive ways, and at younger ages.

THE COOL FACTOR

Department stores first started placing mirrors at children's height in the 1920s, encouraging children to tug at their parents' purse strings. Since then, the under-13 set have come to view themselves as entitled to all the material benefits of the consumer lifestyle.

The "cool factor" has long been an important consideration for kids concerned about their popularity at school. Kids who want the social edge provided by status goods badger their parents for high-priced, name-brand athletic goods, electronics and fashions. The latest video game or pair of running shoes is seen by many – adults and kids alike – as a means of enhancing kids' popularity with their peers.

Parents are feeling more pressure than ever to spend on their children, buying kids overpriced items partly because they worry that without them their kids won' t be seen as cool. Those parents most susceptible to guilt include the divorced, as well as mothers working outside the home.

PESTER POWER

Advertisers spend in excess of US$12 billion yearly trying to attract the attention of young consumers. This investment pays off: research by Corus Entertainment indicates children have memorized between 300 and 400 brand names by the age of 10, and that three-quarters of parents eventually cave in to children' s demands.

Although advertisers have traditionally aimed to encourage children to use their pester power to obtain toys, food and clothing, now a greater variety of merchandise and services – including banks and phone companies – are being pitched directly to the young.

Advertisers are also trying to reach kids earlier, in an attempt to foster life-long brand loyalty. There is an increasing focus on the "tinies" – kids two to four years old. Television shows, video games and interactive websites are a few of the means advertisers use to get kids hooked on particular brands.

Affluenza

A term coined by psychologists for the excessive desire to consume material goods, affluenza describes the unhealthy relationship with money or the pursuit of wealth running rampant across the globe. The young are especially susceptible to this affliction.

What's more, children's sense of entitlement to the material benefits of the "goods life" is often encouraged by their boomer parents. Boomers tend to be enthusiastic consumers themselves, and they find it difficult to say no.

Pampered and Spoiled

When both Mom and Dad are working, guilt makes them feel they need to compensate for the time they're not spending with their children by indulging the kids' every whim. What was once known as spoiling them rotten is now de rigueur, especially in urban and suburban areas. "Keeping up" spurs families to ever-greater spending.

Look at the growing popularity of lavish children's birthday parties. Event management firms are benefiting from the desire among affluent suburban parents to outdo each other in feting their young ones in ways that put yesteryear's pin-the-tail-on-the-donkey affairs to shame. In some cases, the tots are too young to even appreciate the elaborate party thrown in their honour.

One suburban Toronto family threw a Spiderman party for a boy turning six, complete with a mascot in Spiderman garb, a balloon sculptor, a face painter and an entertainer in charge of a hoops game. There was an inflatable castle, a ball pit, and a chef grilling hotdogs and hamburgers, which were served on Spiderman plates and napkins. The price tag? Just over $3,000.

If your little girl opts for a Barbie party – including a chef, popcorn and cotton candy machines, a professional photographer and a Barbie cake – it may set you back as much as $4,500. At least, that was the cost of one two-year-old's birthday bash.

Have the simple joys of party hats, balloons and homemade cake evaporated? These days, time-poor parents are prepared to spare no expense to show their children – and their neighbours – how much they care.

GIRLS INTO PRINCESSES

Every new generation of parents thinks up ways to indulge their children that their own parents would never have dreamed of. A case in point is Club Libby Lu, based in McLean, Virginia, a retail chain targeting 5- to 12-year-old girls. The retailer offers themed fantasy makeover parties and a variety of merchandise that allows the girls to emulate the pop icon of their choice.

The chain invites girls to blend girl-rocker edge with the fun of karaoke and the glamour of the traditional fairytale princess. Tween girls delight in being made over into a Club Libby Lu Rock Pampered Pop Princess in a midriff-baring costume accessorized with a feather boa and wireless microphone headset.

The chain's makeover parties are so popular that Libby Lu's young patrons can face a wait of several months. As with the must-have toy of any given holiday season, it's safe to assume this agonizing waiting period does much to increase the buzz around Club Libby Lu.

For kids and parents wanting to buy into the Libby Lu mystique there are options beyond the parties. The retailer also sells unique and fun merchandise such as the predominantly pink Princess Pilot Case ($29.99), the Hanna Montana Wig ($18.50), High School Musical Microphone ($18), and the Princess Couture Cosmetic Case ($49.99). Prices for Club Libby Lu Style Studio Experience packages run from $22.50 to $35 per kid.

Club Libby Lu's experiential retail concept was so successful that luxury retailer Saks bought up the four-year-old chain in 2003. Saks plans 100 Club Libby Lu shopping centre stores, as well as 150 located in Saks department stores.

This strategy helps Saks tap into the lucrative and underserved tween girl market. In 2000 there were 19.5 million American girls in the 5- to 12-year old age bracket, according to U.S. Census estimates. The buying power of this group is likely to increase as an appetite for spending develops at ever younger ages.

The popularity of princesses amongst modern youngsters is in some ways puzzling. One explanation is that parents fret about a loss of innocence in their information-bombarded children, and embrace the innocuous charm the fairytale princess represents.

Club Libby Lu is not the only company profiting from the surging popularity of princesses. Walt Disney has seen its princess-themed merchandise soar in popularity, as is Barbie Entertainment, created in 2001 by Mattel to drive sales of Princess Barbie dolls. Hollywood cashed in on the trend by releasing a string of princess-themed movies and sequels, including *Disney Princess Stories Volume 3* and *Shrek the Third.*

The popular thirst for fairytale themes may be part of the reason for Club Libby Lu's success, but at the core of the phenomenon is a social trend the chain's founder, Mary Drolet, sought to respond to when she opened her first store in suburban Chicago in 1999. Drolet was previously an executive at Montgomery Ward and specialty retailer Claire's – a chain catering to the same demographic. She concluded there was no shortage of dual-income parents looking for fun ways to connect with their daughters.

BE MY VALENTINE

Just as princesses have been popular with little girls since time immemorial, the Valentine's Day tradition of exchanging cards with classmates is a ritual most of us remember from childhood.

Not all our memories of the event are glowing, however. In the old days, when kids gave cards only to classmates they liked, the less popular felt like pariahs. This system was replaced by the more egalitarian practice of forcing children to give Valentine's Day cards to everyone in the class, friend and bully alike. It could be argued that both systems were more popular with the stationery industry than they ever were with students.

The Valentine's Day card has more recently been reinvented, and age-inappropriate romantic messages have been replaced by phrases like "Have a Nice Day." The term "friend" is more common than the old-fashioned "sweetheart."

More importantly, the imagery of children's Valentine's Day cards has changed. Old-fashioned flowers and hearts have been supplanted by kid icons like SpongeBob SquarePants. Kids are doubtless more excited by a card featuring their favourite animated character than by traditional pseudo-Victorian Valentine's kitsch.

Two trends are at work here. The first reflects the increasing necessity of marketing with kids, rather than to them. While a generation ago children often didn't participate in activities such as buying Valentine's Day cards, in this century they're much more likely to help choose them, and are unlikely to be attracted to cards that mean nothing to them.

The other trend reflects the efforts of marketers to arouse brand awareness in the very young. Promoting a character like SpongeBob SquarePants on Valentine's Day stationery will keep his brand in the hearts and minds of young consumers, who can be expected to demand other kinds of SpongeBob merchandise from their obliging parents.

While no reliable research exists on whether children these days enjoy Valentine's Day more than their parents did, it's likely that modern marketing has done much to make the day more palatable to both parents and kids.

SPA KIDS

North American society has become obsessed with self-pampering. Dwindling amounts of free time and grueling work schedules have made indulgences such as spa treatments seem more like necessities than luxuries.

While pedicures, manicures and mud masques are traditionally adult pleasures, children are one of the fastest growing groups of customers for the North American spa industry. This is not to say that children are shelling out their allowance for spa treatments. Their growing patronage of spas seems rooted in the same social phenomenon that has helped make Club Libby Lu a popular spot for mother-daughter outings. That is, busy parents are always on the lookout for ways to share fun experiences with their kids.

Spas are responding to their increased popularity with the young set by offering treatments geared especially to children's tastes. For example, the Cape Codder Resort & Spa in Hyannis, Massachusetts offers treatments such as a Chocolate Milkshake Pedicure (US$40), Breakout Control Facial ($65), and the Tutti-frutti Manicure Delight ($25).

Girls are naturally the most enthusiastic about getting a head start on beauty treatments, but boys are occasionally coaxed into a hand-soak or pedicure. Men, as it happens, are another fast-growing market for spa services.

Proponents of spa treatments for kids stress the benefits of learning about skin care, nutrition, stress reduction and makeup instruction, and see no irony in applying a mudpack to a nine-year-old girl with perfect skin. Parent-and-child spa visits, after all, have become another way for harried families to enjoy a few precious – and expensive – moments together.

YOUNG METROSEXUALS

Fitness emerged as an obsession for men during the '80s and '90s, but it was not until the current century that popular culture started to take men's grooming seriously. There is now a growing interest in aspects of male grooming that were previously thought unmanly, such as skin care and fashion.

"Metrosexual" became a popular buzzword during the mid-2000s. While many clung to the slovenly ways cultivated by straight males since the dawn of time, others, overtly or covertly, invested in skin care products and expensive shampoos. Since this trend was first noted in the press, it has found its way into the mainstream, especially in urban centres.

Well-educated, financially independent women have higher expectations of potential mates' grooming habits than their mothers did. And men will do whatever is required to attract the opposite sex.

Boys between the ages of 8 and 16 are not so different – or so the marketing thinking goes – and have become the target market for products including deodorants, body washes, hair gels and scents. Not unlike the previously underserved tween girl market, most companies producing grooming products have traditionally disregarded the boys' grooming niche.

Not so today. Young men between the ages of 8 to 18 have been recognized as an important and growing consumer segment by the health and beauty industry, according to the U.S. Market for Teen and Tween Grooming Products. Young men are said to represent a potential market in this category of $2.8 billion by 2008.

Razors, soap, shampoo and other basic grooming products still account for the bulk of personal care items purchased by or for young men. However, marketers have noticed significant opportunities to grow sales of discretionary products such as body sprays and hair colour, which have emerged as the fastest-growing sectors of the teen and tween male personal care market.

While the 21st-century notion of the well-groomed male partly accounts for this trend, these new products also fill a void in the grooming products market. Boys' sense of style is different from their fathers'. In other areas – clothing and snack foods, for instance – boys have come to expect products marketed specifically to them.

The polished image projected by boy bands, with their hip clothes and gelled and spiked hair, is also said to contribute to boys' desire to be well-groomed. For one thing, girls are demanding their male peers look as good as the boys in the bands.

With that kind of pressure, it's no wonder metrosexuality is becoming the norm for the 8 to 16 set.

VIDEO GAME UNIVERSE

One cultural and technological development that's easy for adults to overlook is the explosion of the video game industry. In the first decade of the 21st century the industry was growing 20 per cent annually in the U.S. By 2003, Americans were spending more time playing video games than they spent watching rented DVDs and videos. A U.S. survey showed that 100 per cent of college students had played video games.

Video games fall into a number of different categories. There are the games meant to be installed and played on a personal computer; then there are games that require a separate "platform," such as Sony's Playstation or Microsoft's Xbox. Online competition against friends or complete strangers goes by the awkward acronym of MMORPG (Massively Multiplayer Online Role Playing Game), which has gained a massive following in South Korea, and has greater potential to catch on internationally now that broadband is ubiquitous.

The cultural significance of video games' surging popularity cannot be underestimated. For musicians, selling a song to a game soundtrack rivals landing a spot on a movie soundtrack – partly because of the games' typically massive sales figures, and partly because video game aficionados can be expected to spend as much as 100 hours with the game.

But the tendency of the games to revolve around graphic violence has caused a panic among many parents. Despite the widespread availability of more cerebral strategy games and "God games," in which the player builds and controls a particular environment, the game categories dubbed "fighters" and "shooters" remain wildly popular. It's a fact that point-and-click technology lends itself to aiming at things and hitting them.

Every few months, the media seems to report on a given consumer group calling for the ban of a new ultra-violent game. While studies of children's behaviour come to conflicting conclusions on whether playing violent games makes kids violent, the California State Assembly introduced a bill that would make it illegal for minors to purchase the most violent games. It may be that in a world where parents are too busy to censor their children's preferred forms of entertainment, more legislation will be needed to help prevent videogame culture from taking on increasingly antisocial overtones.

Teens Selling Teens

Teen styles and fads have long proved more or less impossible for any adult to keep up with, and marketers fret about how difficult this group is to reach through conventional advertising. Audiences for television and other media are fragmented, and even when teens are exposed to an ad they often ignore the marketing message.

Marketers hip to what gets teens talking about a product have learned to eschew slick campaigns in favour of guerrilla tactics that capitalize on the power of word-of-mouth among this age group. Teens these days are said to be much more influenced by their peers than their parents were at their age.

Enter Tremor, an arm of Procter & Gamble created in 2001 that enlists teens to plant information about new products in their schools and living rooms by simply chatting about them to friends and family. Tremor's Teen Panel had 230,000 members between the ages of 13 and 19 by the end of 2007.

Tremor more recently developed a service called VocalPoint, a group of women with kids, which grew to over 450,000 within a year of its inception. Tremor boasts that VocalPoint's members represent over 2% of the population of any large U.S. city. Enlisting the help of both Moms and their children in word-of-mouth marketing efforts amounts to a power-packed strategy.

Tremor' s activities help endorse Procter & Gamble products such as CoverGirl cosmetics and Pringle potato chips, but most brands it promotes are not P & G property – AOL, Toyota Motor and Coca-Cola among them.

How does Tremor's Teen Panel work? Through web banner ads and email invitations, the company encourages teens to resister for the chance to win a free DVD player or another hot item. To single out the teens most likely to act as effective missionaries, Tremor's registration questionnaire asks how many friends, acquaintances and family members they communicate with every day. A Tremor teen has about 150 names on their buddy list, while an average teen has a mere 25.

The most social prospects, roughly 10 per cent of those who apply, are invited to join the network. Like many Internet survey sites aimed at adults,

Tremor entices them by offering the opportunity to influence companies. Then there's the appeal of finding out about new products before their friends do. To keep them interested, Tremor sends them token gifts like shampoo, coupons, exclusive music mixes and cheap watches.

Tremor kids aren't necessarily the coolest kids in school. Marketers have learned not to chase after early adopters, who may cotton on to a product early in its life cycle, but can't be relied on to talk about it. Hipsters don't want others copying them, either. But gregarious Tremor teens can be counted on to spread the word about a new shampoo, snack food or even motor oil. (Valvoline hired Tremor to get teens over 16 talking about their product.)

And talk about it they do, on an epic scale – at home, in the school cafeteria, on their cell phones and, most importantly, online.

Of course, word-of-mouth marketing is nothing new. Pharmaceutical companies long ago realized how helpful doctors could be in promoting their products. But Tremor is using word-of-mouth on a scale never seen before. Kids aren't coached, but rather encouraged to feel free to talk to friends. Follow-up takes the form of random phone interviews that track changes in brand image and awareness.

The rise in the popularity of products talked up by Tremor teens is said to more than justify Procter & Gamble's investment. Sales of CoverGirl makeup reportedly rose 10 per cent in markets where groups of Tremor girls were sent a booklet of makeup tips and a round tin containing $1-off coupons.

Not all of Tremor's efforts have been successful, however. A Tampax feminine care "learner's kit" went out to teen girls who already knew all about feminine care, and the effort flopped. Valvoline was hawked to one fifteen-year-old who didn't even have his learner's permit.

The teens themselves are sometimes leery of their role in the Tremor scheme, and are not always at ease handing out samples to their friends. And when kids start to think they're being manipulated by corporations, they're capable of spreading some very negative word-of-mouth.

Tremor's efforts have also been know to raise the ire of parents, some of whom feel their children are being manipulated to sell products without their knowledge or consent. It's a fact that many teens involved in the word-of-mouth marketing effort are not even aware they're taking part in a marketing campaign.

These issues may have influenced Tremor's decision to introduce its

VocalPoint initiative in 2006, targeting mothers rather than more impressionable teens. According to Tremor, an average mom talks to five people daily, while a "connector" – the social type of mom Tremor seeks to enlist – talks to as many as 25. This number of contacts pales in comparison to the social teen's list of 150. Still, it's safe to say that, even in the Kidopoly era, moms' spending decisions carry more clout than those of their teenage children.

Keeping In Touch: Texting

Cell phone users over the age of 30 often find text messaging more appealing in principle than in practice – it may seem a painfully slow way to communicate ideas that could more quickly and eloquently be expressed in an old-fashioned voice message. But the popularity of texting among teens is such that it has developed its own complex lexicon of symbols and abbreviations to speed up the exchange.

This new shorthand first evolved in Internet chat rooms. Acronyms like LOL (laughing out loud), IMHO (in my humble opinion) and TMI (too much information) now even crop up in everyday speech. Smileys or emoticons, like the ever-popular happy face, help bring the nuances of face-to-face conversation to textual exchanges. Text messaging requires even greater brevity than online chat, speeding the growth of this form of slang.

Many of these expressions are known only to the initiated, cementing the new idiom's popularity among teens. As far as most adults are concerned, the common parlance of text messaging might as well be a secret code. Parents will find this list of popular acronyms useful in decoding their children's text messages.

aeap	As early as possible	gal	Get a life	np	No problem
afaik	As far as I know	gbh	Great big hug	otoh	On the other hand
ayt	Are you there?	gtg	Got to go	p911	Parent alert
b4n	Bye for now	hf	Have fun	pir	Parent in room

brb	Be right back	imo	In my opinion	prw	Parents are watching
cyr ma	Call your mother	ilu	I love you	ptb	Please text back
cul8r	See you later	jik	Just in case	ringl8	Running late
dk	Don't know	jk	Just kidding	rme	Rolling my eyes
eod	End of discussion	jw	Just wondering	ruok	Are you okay?
em?	Excuse me?	kpc	Keeping parents clueless	weg	Wicked Evil Grin
f2f	Face to face	mos	Mom over shoulder	yt	You there?
fwiw	For what it's worth	nmu	Not much, you?	zzzzzzzz	Sleeping

Facilitating the texting phenomenon is the overwhelming popularity of portable phones. By the first quarter of 2008, worldwide cell phone sales had reached 300 million units. Three billion people – nearly half the world's population – had become cell phone users.

Many parents give their kids a cell phone, both to keep in touch and to keep track of their whereabouts. In 2007, The Nielsen Company reported that 35 per cent of tween owned a mobile phone. Analysts predict over 80 per cent of Americans ages 5 to 24 will own a cell phone by 2010.

Kids used cell phones for a variety of activities, including surfing the Internet and downloading videos, music and games – not to mention making the occasional voice call. As the cell phone evolves into a handheld computer, the younger generations enthusiastically explore new uses for their phones, developing more complex private lives in the process.

The Generations

Millennials (also known as Generation Y, Echo Boomers, Net Gen)	Homeland Generation (also known as Generation Z, New Silent Generation)
Born 1980 – 2000	Born 2001 – present
Came of age around the turn of the millennium. Individual, optimistic, empowered, innovative.	Growing up with Internet-enabled technologies in a post-9/11 world.
Behaviour influenced by doting parents and structured lives. Paradoxical behaviour: e.g., they smoke although they know the dangers.	Digital technology integrated into all aspects of their lives. They expect to be able to consume media when and where they want.
Primary influencers of retail today	Global interactions

How They Shop

Just as teens' enthusiasm for Internet chat and text messaging is changing the way we communicate, teenagers play a major role in determining the world's tastes, from fashion to music to movies to technology. Most importantly, young shoppers have more buying power than ever before. Their power to decide what's cool can make or break both brands and retailers.

Younger consumers are innovators when shopping for technology, but imitators when it comes to fashion, following trends dictated by favourite celebrities. They may be innovative, but they're still concerned about belonging and conforming to the norms and styles of their social group.

Teens tend to be social beings that rely on their connections with friends, and often look to friends for approval. This peer approval is more important to them than brand. By contrast, their boomer parents are deliberate shoppers who are more inclined to rely on brand trust.

A few facts about the younger shopper's habits:

- Teens are spending more than ever.
- They tend to spend money in good times and bad, being largely unaffected by economic changes.
- Shopping is a social experience.

- Most shopping is recreational, for items like clothes, books and DVDs.
- Stores that want to capture this market need to be places where younger shoppers can have fun and socialize.
- They spend more on hot brand names (e.g., Air Jordans), but are price-sensitive when shopping for style rather than brand (e.g., hoodies).
- This generation is very sensitive to their retail environment. Colour, décor, and music are elements that can attract their business.

Retailers determined to hang on to a significant portion of the teen market need to work overtime to keep up with this group's constantly evolving mindset.

TEEN STYLE

Teens embrace a wide range of personal style. They may change looks in the course of 24 hours: casual for day, sexy and sophisticated for night. Girls put slightly more emphasis on style than boys, and are more likely to feel that what they wear reflects who they are.

Teens like to try whatever's hot, especially when it's in limited supply. Taking their fashion cues from movie stars, TV stars, pop stars and DJs, they shop at a range of retailers to find the looks they're after – thrift stores and discounters in addition to department and specialty stores.

Generally, favourite brands are the same for both boys and girls. Students most often shop for the brands they see as the most fashionable.

At the start of this century, Gap was perhaps the most popular shopping destination for teen fashions. Then attention shifted to specialty retailers like Abercrombie & Fitch, which wooed teens with preppy all-American looks. Then teens developed a preference for European-inspired designs and the hip-hop styles offered by stores like Pacific Sunwear's d.e.m.o. concept, and Abercrombie's market share sagged. American Eagle Outfitters rose to prominence in the second half of the decade as the retailer proved successful at giving teen shoppers what they want.

Frequent shifts in attitudes toward fashion underline the fickleness of the teen market. Any retailer hoping to maintain its edge with this age group needs to work extra hard to maintain its popularity. Proactive teen retailers work at keeping in touch with teens through customer feedback, grass-roots marketing and by studying the chat rooms hosted on the company's websites.

In line with overall shopping trends, many teens are more concerned with good prices than fashion. Discounters that offer both current styles and the perception of low prices, like Target, are increasingly sought out by value-conscious teens.

MARKETING TO TEENS

Predicting youth trends is more difficult than ever. Fads come and go in the blink of an eye, and trends are dictated by teens themselves, not by manufacturers or designers.

Teens can distinguish what's genuinely original from the falsely hip, the way they can distinguish real violence from movie violence. And the buzz about what's cool and what's over travels between them more rapidly than ever, thanks to cell phones and instant messaging.

Keeping up with youth trends requires non-stop research and communication with teens, because teens place a premium on authenticity. Need it be said that teens hate being condescended to?

Advertisers face an uphill battle, because teens are generally skeptical of advertising, and have a knack for ignoring messages even in ads they notice. In addition, slick ad campaigns often turn off early adopters. Advertisers trying to imbue a product with the coveted "cool factor" face a difficult task.

This is not to say that all attempts to get teens' attention are doomed to failure. Guerrilla marketing campaigns incorporating street posters and stickers have been used effectively by skateboard companies and upstart clothing labels that sell to fashion forward youth.

Vans Triple Crown Series running shoes boosted sales exponentially by building a strong link between Vans and sports that teens find cool and take seriously, such as skateboarding, snowboarding and BMX.

Heightened interactivity characterizes successful teen web sites, which cater to teen tastes by being quick loading and easy to use, incorporating cutting-edge technology, rich audio, animation and video. One popular teen site, alloy.com, provides celebrity blogs, fashion tips and links to social networking sites such as Facebook. In addition, the site features surveys that have teens rank their favourite celebrities and give information on their habits and preferences. Advertisers – including Johnson & Johnson, LG and Universal Studios – account for most of alloy.com' s revenues.

Claire's

One of the first chains to successfully tap into the increasingly lucrative tween market was Claire's. Claire's Accessories focuses on 7- to 17-year-old tween and teen girls, providing fun merchandise and an upbeat environment. The affordable merchandise is inspired by the older teens and pop stars that are tweens' fashion role models.

Claire's savvy marketers monitor the media and gather data from their website to determine which celebrities and looks girls love. The company tests items in-store to evaluate their market power before taking them company-wide. New merchandise continually flows into the stores, encouraging customers to visit frequently for the latest looks.

Branding is central to Claire's strategy. The company has its own private label cosmetics lines to make optimal use of the franchise. The Claire's formula, constantly adapted to changing demographics, accounts for 70 per cent of the company's sales.

Claire's Stores, Inc. also operates a chain called Icing By Claire's, which picks up where Claire's leaves off. Icing sells costume jewelry to women aged 17 to 27 – the older sisters of Claire's target customers. The chain attracts the older demographic with sexier, more glamorous merchandise, including jewelry, cosmetics, leather goods and stationery.

Claire's has established a colourful, highly visible presence in shopping centres across North America, maintaining its popularity by keeping on top of the trends and offering stylish merchandise at affordable prices. Aggressive expansion in Europe, a successful joint-venture in Japan and franchise stores throughout the Middle East, Russia, South Africa and Turkey have reinforced the company's reputation as a leader in selling to the teen and tween market.

Petopoly: Kids for the Kidless

For those who can't or don't want to have children, especially urban singles and couples, pets increasingly provide a focus for people's care-giving instincts.

Dogs, the pet of choice for even condo dwellers, are said to give unconditional love and need a lot of looking after – just like children.

Modern pet owners are eager to give their furry charges a taste of the good life, leading to a proliferation in high-end pet services, accommodations and accessories. Like parents, pet owners are expected to open their wallets to raise their adopted puppy in the appropriate fashion. As a result, Canada's pet industry has surpassed $3 billion in annual sales.

The growing tendency to lavish expensive treats on pets bears a striking resemblance to the largesse with which people are raising their children.

Does this mean people these days treat their pets as well as their children – or as badly?

Pet Vacations

The term "kennel" strikes the ears of the modern pet owner as barbaric. Petsmart, the No. 1 pet supply chain in the U.S., has stepped in to provide more humane temporary accommodations for people who want their animal friends to enjoy an almost human level of comfort while on vacation.

Petsmart began boarding pets in 2001, and has a long-term goal of installing instore PetsHotels in up to 20 per cent of its stores. Animal guests checked into a basic atrium room (about US$21, depending on the location) enjoy meals and walks included in the price of accommodation.

It's also possible to upgrade to a more lavish suite, complete with a television showing animal movies. These dog-oriented facilities feature a "Bone Booth," which gives pet owners the opportunity to chat on the phone with their dogs, with some help from Petsmart staff.

In addition to day camp services offered inside PetSmart's PetsHotels, the retailer is opening Doggie Day Camps in stores that lack overnight facilities. This initiative aims to give time-starved pet owners another reason to pass up the competition.

For cat lovers there are separately located kitty condos. These feline resort facilities keep guests purring by offering interactive play sessions dubbed TLC time.

The rapid growth of the pet hospitality industry can best be explained by guilt: people feel bad about leaving their surrogate children in unfamiliar surroundings, and do their best to compensate by pampering them. The modern pet owner is as guilt-ridden as the modern parent.

DOGGY DAYCARE

Urban Dog, an 7,500-square-foot "Urban Canine Oasis" that opened in Toronto in 2003, embodies the increasingly indulgent approach to pet pampering. Dog spa and daycare facilities, such as New York's Dog Hotel, started up in the U.S. years earlier, and will no doubt continue to proliferate in both countries.

Urban Dog offers play areas with playground equipment, cushioned athletic flooring and the unique Nanny Cam, which streams video from the dogs' play area to the Internet. Anxious dog owners can log in from work and watch their pet making new friends, or instruct a caregiver to give the canine some extra attention. At CAD$37.50 a day, sending your pet to Urban Dog five days a week adds up to $9,750 a year, or the cost of sending a child to private school.

Caring for pets, clearly, is not the miserly affair it once was. Our idea of what now constitutes a reasonable vet's bill is telling: not long ago vets mostly spayed and neutered animals, administered a limited range of shots and put sick pets to sleep. Nowadays, expensive procedures like bone grafts and chemotherapy are becoming the norm, as people unwilling to let go of their beloved pet enlist medical specialists to help them enjoy more time together.

NINE LIVES

As not even modern surgical techniques will make an animal live forever, the option of cloning a beloved pet holds obvious appeal. In the fall of 2004, Genetic Savings & Clone, Inc., (tagline: "Gene banking and cloning of exceptional pets") accepted more than US$50,000 to clone a woman's aging cat. The result was Little Nicky, the world's first commercially cloned feline, the genetic twin of a 17-year-old Maine Coon cat.

Headquartered in Sausalito, California, Genetic Savings & Clone was started by Arizona billionaire John Sperling, whose ambition was to clone his favourite dog. The cat-cloning program, dubbed "Nine Lives Extravaganza," debuted in 2004, and by early 2005 the price for this service had dropped to a more affordable $32,000. The company stated its plans to offer dog cloning in 2005.

However, the company's fate shows there are in fact limits to how much people will spend on their pets. Only two cloned cats were sold, and Genetic Savings & Clone closed its doors in late 2006.

In an age that welcomes lavish spending on furry companions, it's no surprise there are a few people in the world willing to pay tens of thousands to extend a feline love affair. What nature takes away, biotechnology can give back. But clearly pet cloning will not catch on until it can be done at prices within limits pet lovers see as reasonable – and those limits are constantly expanding.

Canine Couture

Maintaining a stylish abode is a bigger priority than ever. But how to keep your home looking good when, despite your best efforts, your pet can make such a mess?

Fortunately, pet ownership is a matter several home décor gurus have turned their attention to. Julia Szabo's Animal House Style, for instance, provides tips on living stylishly with a variety of pet species.

In some circles, both pets and their accoutrements are expected to complement your home's design scheme. Designer Karim Rashid launched a line of pet accessories called Dxg Bxne, and IKEA has its own range of pet products, including toys, scratching posts and beds.

Boutique products for the well-loved canine include biscotti, fortune cookies and truffles, leather jackets and even four-poster beds. Status seekers have long since discovered it's easy to spend a bundle on items like the Louis Vuitton dog collar. Being a pet has never been so luxurious.

Pet-People vs. People-People

Attitudes toward pet care have shifted radically over the past generation or two, and the pet-indulgent behaviour once reserved for the very rich is becoming the norm.

Not everyone is comfortable with this development. Some tacitly believe people who lavish love on animals tend to be insensitive to the plight of their fellow human beings.

This view is not necessarily supported by rigorous research. However, an article in Canada's *National Post* contained a telling anecdote about a recently divorced mother. She claimed her ex-husband, who had custody of the family dog, was trying to deduct the cost of canine care from his child-support payments.

Pets are a more expensive proposition than in the past, and a more important part of the family unit than ever.

CHAPTER 6

LUXURY FOR ALL

FOR THE LOVE OF LUXURY

THE last decade has seen the rise of a new class of consumer: people with easy access to abundant credit, who make saving a low priority, and who treat luxuries as necessities. Even exclusive brand names once reserved for the privileged few are attainable, and have even become indispensable to the urban high life.

The love of luxury has asserted itself as the North American, and increasingly international, norm. Income growth, low interest rates, and dwindling prices for many goods thanks to cheap imports means that even the poorest people feel entitled to a certain level of indulgence.

Welcome to the consumer landscape of the 21st century, where luxury goods and services, from spa treatments to designer handbags to lattes to high-end appliances, are all the more desirable because everyone has them. Keeping up with the Joneses never used to look like this.

BUYING HAPPINESS

While the world's elites indulge conspicuously in high-end goods, the average gratification-seeking consumer lives in a state of continual frustration. In her book *The Overspent American*, author Juliet B. Schor notes that over a quarter of people earning more than $100,000 say they can't afford to buy everything they really need.

This shows the meaning of the word "need" is closer to "want" than ever before. Faced with luxury temptations in magazines, TV commercials and shop windows, consumers at every income level are likely to feel that whatever they have isn't enough.

Because people judge themselves in relation to others, any society-wide increase in household income makes little difference in how people feel about themselves. While more money may make people happier temporarily, happiness and self-esteem are closely linked to rank and relative income. You may be happy with your Louis Vuitton purse today, but if your best friend comes to lunch with a new Hermes creation over her shoulder you may start to feel dissatisfied.

THE TRADING UP CULTURE

Society's attitudes toward consumption have evolved as the technologies of manufacturing and selling have developed. Older economies, or producer cultures, were fettered by limited production capacity, and people's material aspirations were tempered by consumer goods' relative scarcity. In today's surplus economy, even those toward the bottom of the earnings ladder may achieve a much more substantial level of material consumption.

The industrial revolution of the 18th century put cheaply manufactured goods in the hands of the masses for the first time. More than two hundred years later, the material needs of average consumers in prosperous Western countries, and increasingly Asia as well, have been amply fulfilled.

Not long ago, consumers primarily wanted goods that filled a material void. With most material "needs" fulfilled, the emphasis has shifted to shopping for things that fulfil emotional desires. Luxury goods have a deeper psychological significance than their more run-of-the-mill equivalents, and this accounts for much of their appeal.

The increased knowledge among middle-class consumers about luxury brands contributes to the widespread desire to trade up for items that have that emotional advantage. People are prepared to pay a premium of between 20 and 200 per cent for perceived higher levels of quality and performance, at least on items that really matter to them.

An avid golfer may be willing to splurge on the best golf clubs money can buy, for example, while trading down on everyday household items by shopping at discounters. New luxury consumers are likely to spend lavishly on home décor and improvements, but may put a lower priority on fashion spending as they remake their kitchens with granite countertops and Sub Zero appliances.

As what used to be aspirational becomes attainable, the ceiling for the high end is pushed even higher. When cashmere became affordable, along came pashmina to fill the aspirational void.

There's also a phenomenon known as the Veblen Effect, named for Thorstein Veblen, the 19th-century American economist who coined the phrases "status-seeking" and "conspicuous consumption." He argued the expense of luxury goods actually makes up part of their value. The idea of the Veblen Effect is that astronomical prices justify big spending, which helps account for the enduring popularity of high-priced goods.

"Veblen goods" are thus extravagances like vintage wines or high-end perfumes, whose attractiveness correlates directly with their price tag. An equally important phenomenon is the Counter-Veblen Effect, which sees consumer desire increase as prices fall. Stores like Target capitalize on the Counter-Veblen Effect by selling formerly expensive stuff at bargain prices.

Everyone, including the rich, likes a good deal. But when luxuries that were once inaccessible to the masses become commonplace, luxury aficionados seek out even more expensive goods that have the emotional appeal that only truly aspirational items possess. This is why both old-fashioned "exclusive" luxury brands and high-end brands with a wide following are thriving in today's luxury-mad marketplace.

From Class to Mass

Luxury concepts typically evolve from highly exclusive to widely aspirational to commonplace – in other words, from class to mass. Yesterday's luxury is today's necessity.

The television set is a good example. The first television stations started broadcasting in the late 1920s, and by 1936 there were about 2,000 TV sets in use around the world. By 1948, over a million U.S. homes had TV. At this stage TV was a futuristic luxury, enjoyed chiefly by the rich and the upper middle class, and by friends and relations who dropped in to gather around these scarce sets for popular shows.

By 1960, TV had infiltrated the homes of 90 per cent of Americans, making the U.S. the world's first TV society. TV was no longer a luxury, and had become an integral part of day-to-day American life – although having more than one set was still a sign of affluence.

In 1978, 98 per cent of American households had TV sets, up from 9 per cent in 1950. Television became such an ingrained part of the U.S. lifestyle that in 1993 a *TV Guide* poll found that one in four Americans would not give up TV even for a million dollars.

The class-to-mass pattern characterizes the adoption of all kinds of gadgets, from microwave ovens to cell phones to flat panel TVs. Thanks to phenomena such as technological advances in manufacturing and global overcapacity, combined with the downward pressure on prices often described as the Wal-Mart effect, what starts out as a novelty for the wealthy soon finds its way into the lives of just about everyone.

For instance, colour TV is now commonplace even in the slums of Rio de Janeiro, where civic services such as garbage removal and electricity can be unreliable. Nonetheless, soap operas are wildly popular in Brazil, and even the poorest in society feel entitled to watch them.

The television set's transformation from luxury item to household necessity was slow by today's standards. The more rapid flow of information combined with adaptable manufacturing processes and constant worldwide innovation mean that the time lag between a product's debut on the consumer market and its reincarnation in cheap versions for the masses is ever briefer. People quickly find out everything there is to know about new products on the Internet, increasing pressure on manufacturers to produce reasonably-priced versions of formerly high-end products to satisfy demand. This acceleration of the product cycle applies as much to fashion as it does to consumer electronics.

The Evolution of the Luxophile

In the decades following the Second World War, the earnings of Americans in almost every income bracket increased at roughly the same rate. That changed in the early 1970s. Since then, only the very richest Americans have enjoyed significant income growth.

Wealthy Americans largely spend what they earn, setting standards of consumption for the entire nation. The global reach of American movies and television means that rich Americans are simultaneously shaping perceptions of the good life for consumers around the world.

As America's wealthy buy and pay more, those in less affluent households seek to emulate their big-spending ways. The home renovation and décor industries are booming as people fill their spacious abodes with home theatre systems and renovate their kitchens with high-end appliances.

In the old days, luxury was closely associated with ostentation, prestige and high price. More recently, consumers have been moving upscale in large numbers, while luxury goods move downscale. This has led to the "massification" of traditional luxury brands, and a shift in the very definition of luxury. Marketers have attached luxury associations to many products that never used to be in the luxury league. Packaging and advertising are now liberally sprinkled with adjectives like platinum, premium, gourmet and pro.

The fact that such "exclusivity" is now widely available has done little to diminish its sparkle. When everyone can afford luxury, luxury becomes that much more desirable, thanks to people's psychological need to keep up with the Joneses and assert their status in society. There will always be those who reach beyond luxury's more mundane levels, showcasing their superiority through ostentatious display. If the neighbours drive a Mercedes, there's always Bentley.

True Luxury vs. New Luxury

The last couple of decades have seen a decline in traditional luxury, while mass-market luxury has caught fire. Companies that offer luxuries made by hand in Western countries are now few and far between.

For decades, Hermès manufactured its sought-after accessories in France, in much the same way it has for generations, guaranteeing the brand a dedicated following and a unique market niche. In the 21st century, the company started outsourcing the sewing of its iconic scarves to Mauritius. Meanwhile, Louis Vuitton announced plans to build a shoe factory in India, while Armani embraced Chinese labour.

In the old days, luxury goods sold in small volumes in exclusive stores to a few well-heeled customers. This consumer market was pyramid-shaped, widening toward the bottom as prices declined and products were more widely available. In North America, the consumers who once formed the vast middle of this pyramid are migrating upwards, trading middle-market products for premium goods.

The market these days is increasingly shaped like an hourglass, with consumers focusing their attention on either the very expensive or the very cheap. Retailers who traditionally did their main business with the middle market – most department stores, for instance – are finding it difficult to position themselves in a way that consumers can relate to. The retail landscape now lends itself to polarized shopping behaviour.

For nearly all luxury brands, old-fashioned craftsmanship has been replaced by the savvy marketing of more cheaply manufactured goods to a growing international customer base. Brands maintain their luxury image through advertising, but in many cases the glamorous goods they're selling are relatively affordable and widely available. While in some respects new luxury goods remain aspirational, they are simultaneously achievable, and play a larger role in the lives of more consumers.

The other significant shift that has occurred since true luxury gave way to new luxury is that people's motivations for having luxury in their lives have changed. For many it is not so much a goal as a necessity. Today's consumer places a higher value on well-being and a personal sense of satisfaction than the consumer of a generation ago, and these tend to be the values that help them rationalize their expensive indulgences.

The famous tagline "Because you're worth it" has a lot to answer for. A luxury purchase, whether a Hermès handbag, a bottle of premium extra virgin olive oil or a BMW, provides reassurance to the buyer that he or she is a full participant in our consumer society. Buying luxury goods allows the purchaser to become the equal to the friends, co-workers and celebrities partaking in the same kind of indulgence.

BRIDGING THE LUXURY GAP

The Forbes annual tracking guide to the world's richest people estimated there were over 1,000 billionaires worldwide in 2008, up from only 140 a mere 20 years earlier. Sales of luxury goods, in the billions for the first decade of the millennium, are projected to exceed $1 trillion in 2010.

The super-rich have created a growing market for breathtakingly expensive items, such as jewel-encrusted watches and cell phones with pricetags in the hundreds of thousands of dollars. But it's the world's middle class that is consuming luxury merchandise like never before. Today's average consumer feels entitled to luxury no matter what the economic climate.

Recent data from Canada and the U.S. indicates that despite substantial income growth among society's richest households over the last couple of decades, middle class incomes have hardly budged, when adjusted for inflation. The growing gap between the rich and the not-so-rich is not necessarily obvious to the casual observer, however, because the middle class can now afford many of the things that were once the preserve of the wealthy. While the income gap spreads, the luxury gap narrows.

While the primary purchasers of traditional luxury goods and services are still those with household incomes of $200,000 and more, marketers have begun to tap the desire for luxury in a broader range of consumers by infusing previously ordinary categories with an element of luxury. The $4 Starbucks latte is one example.

Brands that were previously inaccessible to anyone but the super-rich have also introduced more affordable product extensions that allow a greater number of consumers a taste of the good life. The increased availability of luxury products and services at lower price points has created a democratization of luxury. For example, cookware and cutlery by Viking Range Corporation is accessible to consumers who can't afford $5,000 for a Viking range.

Luxury companies are trying to reach the "mass affluent" – the upper-middle-class and middle-class – who crave affordable luxuries, especially when the economy is shaky. "New luxury" goods allow less affluent consumers to experience higher levels of quality and aspiration. Products like this keep selling when the economy is uncertain because they fulfill powerful emotional needs.

This democratization of luxury has created a difficult situation for purveyors of luxury items. The elusiveness of true exclusivity has been described as an "existential crisis in the world of luxury goods."

Six Stages of Luxury

The rich embrace many approaches to luxury spending, depending on their tastes, interests, lifestyle – and when they acquired their riches. Here are six approaches to luxury spending, from crass to refined to avoiding it altogether.

Acquisitive Luxury: The first and broadest level of the luxury pyramid. This approach to luxury spending is embraced by the new rich, such as rock stars and recent millionaires in Moscow and the Middle East. Recently acquired disposable cash is spent indiscriminately on tasteless, flashy items that wear their conspicuousness on their sleeve.

Inquisitive Luxury: These consumers understand quality and exercise a modicum of taste and discretion in purchasing food, wine, fashion and home furnishings. They are aware of the difference between the best single-malt Scotch and an inferior blend. They have enough disposable income to satisfy their desires, and impress their peers primarily with their confidence in the rightness of what they purchase.

Authoritative Luxury: Fads hold no interest to this rarefied group. Able to afford whatever they want, they are so confident in their tastes that they create their own fashion. These consumers shun regular stores and prefer shopping in specialized ateliers, such as Paul Smith's London Curiosity Shop, an idiosyncratic retail concept offering clothes, art and furnishings. These knowledgeable rich love acquiring things other people don't know about yet, and are the group most likely to identify the next big thing.

Meditative Luxury: Much has been written in the past decade about the increasing value placed on experiences as opposed to retail goods. Consumers at this fourth stage have everything they need and regard luxury as time, in particular time spent on learning and "experience collecting." A Mount Everest climb or African safari involving all the best equipment might appeal to a consumer in this group. They're not impressed by brand names or Michelin star ratings, and have long grown out of ostentatious pretension. They may spend much of their time on a private acreage, and have clothes tailor-made because it's simpler than shopping.

Enlightened Luxury: This is the pyramid's tip, the hardest stage to reach, inhabited by a tiny elite of ultra-consumers. They have discerning taste, collecting both the tangible and intangible, and only buy one piece of anything: the very best example of its kind. Their approach to consumption is so selective that sometimes they and the seller are among the few people in the world who appreciate the true value of their acquisitions.

Anti-Luxury: This evolving sixth stage has also been termed "Nu Austerity" – a tendency among intellectual tastemakers to jump off the luxury bandwagon altogether. The Joneses are too boring to bother keeping up with, "status" fashions no longer seem cool, and downsizing has become chic. Having owned an abundance of stuff, these consumers are bored with it, and couldn't care less about impressing their peers. This trend raises the possibility that "conspicuous abstention" may be a trend the retail industry will need to watch, particularly as Generations X and Y take the place of the baby boomers over the next couple of decades.

Consumer Mindsets

Of course, the ongoing popularity of status items like the Louis Vuitton handbag shows that such goods are still aspirational for most consumers. For people whose earnings may not be at the top of the income pyramid, luxury spending is driven by five distinct mindsets. Each mindset responds to different value propositions and marketing messages.

"**Luxury Is Functional**." These consumers buy luxury products for their superior functionality and quality. Consumers in this segment tend to be older and wealthier, and are willing to spend more on things that will last and have enduring value: luxury cars, artwork or vacations. They do extensive pre-purchase research and their purchase decisions are more logical than impulsive or emotional.

"**Luxury Is a Reward**." Consumers in this group often use luxury items as status symbols to say "I've made it." They desire to be seen as successful, and purchase conspicuous items such as luxury cars and exclusive homes. Widely recognized luxury brands are popular with this segment. At the same time, they're concerned about appearing lavish or hedonistic, and want to purchase "smart" luxury items that won't invite criticism. "Acceptable exclusivity" appeals to this group.

"**Luxury is Experience**." As affluent baby boomers enter their retirement years, some de-emphasize material goods in favour of new experiences and ephemeral indulgences, such as spa treatments and adventure vacations. They are often ex-yuppies who, surrounded by a surfeit of material goods acquired through the years, decide it's time to simplify. They aim to pursue a more relaxed, uncluttered lifestyle by letting go of conspicuous consumption.

"**Luxury Is Indulgence**." These consumers are often younger and are more predominantly male than the other groups. For them the purpose of owning luxury is to be lavish and self-indulgent. They will pay a premium for goods that express their individuality and make others notice. They're not particularly concerned with quality, and aren't worried about being criticized. They enjoy luxury for the way it makes them feel, and are likely to make impulse purchases.

"**Luxury Is Comforting.**" The least wealthy group, these consumers are typically younger urbanites. They feel entitled to small indulgences on a daily basis, so any form of budgeting feels like privation. Some are PUPpies – Poor Until Payday. While not really poor, consumers in this group have no savings and don't make enough to support their frequent splurges on small luxuries like slick magazines, lattes and clothes. They don't keep track of where their money goes, maxing out credit cards and sometimes taking out payday loans to make ends meet. They are the most likely to indulge in "retail therapy" or buy on impulse, often with the goal of making themselves feel better.

OLDER & RICHER

Early baby boomers have already moved into the 55-to-74-year-old age category, bringing a surge in the number of households headed by older people with incomes of $100,000 and more. This means a sharp rise in the demand for goods and services, including health care, travel and luxury products. Given boomers' free-spending ways, forward-thinking marketers have already started targeting this lucrative segment.

In the future, the market will be robust for expensive and highly customized products and services, because older consumers are likely to be weary of ordinary products and ready for something different. This may create the unprecedented phenomenon of trend-setting behaviour by the 55-to-74 set. Trends established in luxury products will be widely reproduced in much cheaper knock-offs, which will appeal to consumers who wish to emulate the styles of the rich without copying their spending habits.

Specialized health care services are benefiting greatly from the rising numbers of affluent older people, as are cosmetic procedures, spa treatments and products that promise to reverse the aging process. There will be an increase in the demand for non-standard therapies for both the physical and mental conditions afflicting older people. Other trends include older consumers purchasing second or third residences, while others prefer to purchase luxury goods or take extended vacations.

Not Flaunting It

Contrary to popular belief, the rich often don't look rich. Strictly speaking, the more you spend on looking rich, the less you're worth.

Many of us confuse wealth with income, whereas wealth is what you accumulate in assets, not what you make or spend. This divides consumers into two distinct groups: wealth accumulators and hunter-gatherers. Wealth accumulators aren't just better off financially, they feel better about their lives.

Those who would like to accumulate wealth should ask themselves four questions:

- Does your household operate on an annual budget? Most millionaires have a budget, even those who don't invest first (a minimum of 15 per cent of their annual income).
- Do you know how much your family spends each year on food, clothing and shelter? Accumulators know exactly how much they spend on everything. Hunter-gatherers don't keep track.
- Do you have a defined set of daily, weekly, monthly, annual and life-time goals? The most satisfied wealthy people don't just have financial goals, they're also clear about what they want in life.
- Do you spend a lot of time planning your financial future? Wealth accumulators spend nearly twice the number of hours per month planning their investments as those who depend on their large incomes do – yet they spend much less time worrying about their financial well-being.

The two things that truly wealthy people value more than financial planning are entertaining close friends and spending time with their children or grandchildren.

Marketing Luxury

Not all luxury is created equal. Or perhaps we should say not all luxury is marketed in the same way.

Luxury items are promoted according to one of three basic strategies:

Affordable Luxuries. The winner in this category is the $4 Starbucks latte. Through shrewd marketing, Starbucks managed to create an aura of luxury around its coffees, which North Americans had previously never treated as a luxury at all. Many other "gourmet" food products and personal care items, not to mention the disposable fashions of chains like H&M, fall into the affordable luxury category. There is considerable potential for growth in the affordable luxury market because many consumers quickly become habitual rather than occasional purchasers.

Essential Luxuries. These items, once the province of the wealthy, have become must-haves for even middle-income consumers. The kitchens of mid-range condominiums in major urban centres, for instance, often come with granite countertops and stainless steel appliances as standard equipment, although these features were reserved for rich homeowners just a decade ago. The Louis Vuitton handbag, once carried only by socialites, is now a favourite of office workers.

Distinctive Luxuries. Products in this category are the last bastion of luxury as it used to be defined: top-of-the-line, very exclusive products available to a select group of people through limited channels. Hermès, which manufacturers its luxury goods using traditional low-volume methods, stopped taking orders for its Birkin tote bag in 2002 because the waiting list had grown too long. Only a company with Hermès's irrefutable cachet can afford to simply say no to clamorous customers. What's more, by doing so the company reinforced its unique position in the Distinctive Luxury niche.

LOUIS VUITTON

No brand bridges the divide between traditional luxury and new luxury better than Louis Vuitton. In 1989, Chairman Bernard Arnault purchased the company and set it on a course to realize its enormous growth potential. Part of parent company LVMH Moët Hennessy Louis Vuitton, the legendary accessory and luggage maker quickly surpassed rivals like Gucci, Hermès and Prada to become the world's most profitable luxury brand, with operating margins as high as 45 per cent.

Louis Vuitton products provide consumers everything they crave from a high-end brand. The company's long history as a purveyor of traditional luxury goods gives it a romance few newer companies can match, yet at the same time it churns out eye-catching new styles, courtesy of chief designer Marc Jacobs, a New Yorker originally associated with the grunge look. The shoe line he introduced accounts for 15 per cent of Vuitton's sales and is a big draw for younger customers.

Then there's Louis Vuitton's legendary quality, including a lifetime repair guarantee, which even in the luxury industry is exceptional – many customers of competing brands are dismayed at how astronomical repair expenses become part of the cost of ownership of a high-end handbag. Every detail of a Louis Vuitton bag is carefully scrutinized, from the durability of the zipper to the flawless leather trim.

Just as important, the company maintains strict controls on distribution, and its items never go on sale. You'll never find a Louis Vuitton bag at a steep discount at Target – and this reassures customers they're worth paying a hefty premium for. A significant part of the company's strategy rests on its ability to convince customers they belong to an exclusive club, entrance to which cannot be had at a discount.

And Louis Vuitton customers are enthusiastic club members. Loyalty to the brand is exceptional, with many customers building collections of these treasured accessories. The company encourages customers to move up from the classic brown-and-tan style to newer lines such as the Suhali goatskin bags, which on average sell for more than US$2,000.

The global proliferation of the monogrammed bags is assured as the company conquers new markets. In the early 2000s Japanese customers accounted for over half of the company's revenues, but the bags have been gaining popularity in the U.S. and in countries with rapidly growing economies, such as India and China.

One of the threats to the brand's success is the booming business in counterfeit bags, largely centred in China. The brand's cachet, however, leads the Chinese themselves to spurn the fakes, which are mostly exported or sold to tourists.

Louis Vuitton is investing more heavily in advertising than in previous years, building campaigns that associate the products with celebrities and supermodels. The brand's popularity shows that trading old-fashioned exclusivity for worldwide dominance can be a profitable business.

On the other hand, the ubiquitousness of the Louis Vuitton bag – which had an awe-inspiring air of exclusivity prior to the company's changing hands in '89 – has irrevocably changed how consumers see the brand. As fashion-conscious girls from middle-income households proudly sport the LV monogram on their way to work, Inquisitive and Authoritative Luxury consumers (described above) are no doubt looking to other brands for the cachet needed to impress their more discerning peers.

DISPOSABLE LUXURY: FAST FASHION

In a world where many types of clothing are steadily becoming cheaper, increasing numbers of fashion-hungry consumers are abandoning the "investment" approach to dressing. For many, the idea of buying high-quality items and holding onto them forever is passé.

These days, those in search of the very latest check out stores like H&M, Zara and Mango, where style is available at throwaway prices. Consumers are embracing the democratic pleasure of clothes so affordable they need be worn only once or twice to justify their cost. And because of their current designs, these clothes mix well with traditional luxury accessories such as Jimmy Choo shoes and Burberry scarves.

Fast fashion stores get up-to-the-minute styles to eager shoppers with astonishing speed. It can take Zara as little as ten days from sketching a new design to delivering the piece of clothing to stores.

Designers at these chains keep on top of the latest fashion trends by attending fashion shows and frequenting nightclubs and other havens of the hip to observe what young, fashion-forward women are wearing. Design teams meet frequently to compare notes on emerging trends.

These retailers understand people have come to view fashion as a disposable commodity, and succeed largely thanks to their superb use of technology and rapid-response manufacturing and distribution. Yet their products remain aspirational: the stylish designs resemble the output of big-name French and Italian fashion houses, but at prices so low that no one need view the clothes as an investment.

Fast fashion has even been accepted by big-name designers who in past decades catered to the luxury market. Isaac Mizrahi, the creator of a couture line, was hired by U.S. discounter Target to design an affordable collection including $15 cardigans and $25 trench coats. The collaboration proved so successful that Mizrahi became something of a permanent fixture at the retailer. At H&M, a number of big fashion names have designed clothing lines, including Karl Lagerfeld, Stella McCartney, Victor&Rolf and Roberto Cavalli.

There has been a sea change in the way people view these stores, too. Once upon a time, women worked hard to conceal the fact they got their designer styles at knockoff prices. These days, serious fashionistas are quite open about the fact they shop Zara or H&M on a regular basis – in part because the styles at these stores are as likely to be up-to-date as anything at more expensive retailers. And if a shopper saves money by buying an outfit at H&M, she can always put it toward her next pair of Manolo Blahniks.

China, Land of Luxury

Underlying the proliferation of luxury goods and evolving attitudes toward consumption are fundamental changes in the global economy, including the dramatic rise of China's prosperity. In 2005, China surpassed the U.S. as the world's number one consumer of food and industrial goods.

Once rigidly egalitarian, China now has one of the world's widest gaps between rich and poor, and those at the top don't hesitate to embrace every luxury the open market provides. While poverty remains the norm in the countryside, hundreds of millions of urban Chinese are now rich enough to live a lifestyle involving the kind of spending Americans have enjoyed for decades.

Communist leader Mao Zedong died in 1976, and after a two-year power struggle Deng Xiaoping took control of the country, gradually opening its economy to the forces of market competition. Inspired by the astounding economic success of neighbouring countries like Japan, Deng brought capitalism to China in small doses. He turned Shenzen, across the border from Hong Kong, into a special economic zone open to foreign investment. The experiment succeeded beyond optimists' wildest dreams, transforming the city into a thriving boomtown, not to mention the home of China's first McDonald's.

The 1989 massacre of protesters in Tiananmen Square reminded the world that the economic reforms had not enhanced the country's democratic freedoms. The catastrophe also put Deng and his allies on the defensive, as conservative rivals clamoured to reverse the liberalizing of the economy.

Deng briefly disappeared from the public eye, but resurfaced in 1992 with a plan to open up a dozen new special economic zones across the country. Foreign investment poured in, and China embarked on an ambitious course of economic expansion. As a result, China's economy will surpass Japan's by 2015 and that of the U.S. by 2039, predict analysts at Goldman Sachs.

The country has become the world's manufacturing heartland, which has driven down the cost of consumer goods everywhere. Half the planet's clothes are made in China. Home to about a fifth of the world's population, China's cities are burgeoning with consumer goods like plasma TVs and Louis Vuitton handbags. China is now the world's number one market for cell phones.

MADE IN CHINA

The size and speed of China's economic takeoff caught Western manufacturers off guard. In North America and Western Europe, it is no longer economically feasible to manufacture many goods that were profitable just a decade ago.

Some point out that Western manufacturing has in past decades adjusted to influxes of foreign manufactured goods – notably from Japan and Korea. China's impact on manufacturing is on a completely different scale, however.

China is already a huge market for consumer goods, in addition to being an export power. That gives it unparalleled economies of scale.

Manufactured goods from China run the gamut from cheap clothing to furniture to high-end digital electronics, whereas other Asian nations shed labour-intensive work as they industrialized. China can compete both in low wages and high-tech expertise, so its low-priced exports impact almost every retail category.

The Chinese takeover of retail categories happens with unprecedented speed, leaving foreign competitors little time to adjust.

Unlike Japan or Korea, China encourages foreign investment, a significant factor in the country's explosive growth. Foreign investment accounts for 60 per cent of exports and a large share of domestic sales.

Foreign investment gives China easy access to foreign markets. Chinese electronics makers are able to build market share by selling through Wal-Mart without investing as much in advertising and distribution as Japan's Sony or Korea's Samsung did.

North American manufacturers increasingly find themselves unable to compete with Chinese rivals, and many have been forced to shut down. The "China price" for making many kinds of goods is often 30 to 50 per cent less than a product can be manufactured for in the U.S. In some cases, Chinese companies can make items for less than the cost of the raw materials in the West.

Some companies outside China compete by continually modernizing their manufacturing and distribution facilities. Zara, for instance, makes most of its clothes in Spain, importing a growing proportion of its merchandise from Asia. The retailer succeeds because all facets of its operations are ruthlessly efficient, and distribution costs are recouped by the price of the clothes. Zara fashions sold in North America cost more than their equivalents in Europe to offset shipping costs.

Louis Vuitton uses increasing automation to bolster its healthy profit margins. The company keeps its manufacturing base in France, a strategy that works because customers are willing to pay a hefty premium for the brand's made-in-France cachet.

Many brands, however, rely on Chinese plants to manufacture their products at internationally competitive prices. This is an enormously profitable practice, boosting Western companies' return on capital substantially. They increase margins by reducing the cost of making their products, without substantially changing the price they charge North American or European consumers. For many goods – cell phones and shampoo, for instance – the country of manufacture makes little difference to consumers.

This has led marketers to find innovative ways to distinguish their made-in-China products. A toy's packaging might read "Designed in Great Britain," assuring consumers that what they're buying has the emotional appeal of a high-end British-made item – even if it really came from China. Clothing labels still say "Made in Hong Kong" even though Hong Kong was handed over to China in 1997 – presumably because this suggests the items are of higher quality. Marketers can be expected to continue finding ways to counteract the lack of emotional resonance of the phrase "Made in China."

A backlash against Chinese-made products materialized in 2007, when a series of recalls of toys decorated with lead paint and a tainted pet food scandal drew attention to China's lax health and safety standards. Some consumers, especially younger, well-educated ones, now spurn Chinese goods. Luxury goods bearing a Made-in-China label have less cachet than ever, looking more than ever like vulgar counterfeits of the European or North American goods they are in most respects identical to. At the same time, growing consumer distaste for this imported merchandise has had little impact on its popularity, as few would be willing to return to the days when equivalent items cost several times more.

LITTLE EMPERORS

In 1980, China's social planners introduced an edict limiting families to one child each, a policy Beijing claims is partly responsible for raising living standards. It is estimated that at least a fifth of Chinese under age 25, or 100 million people, have been raised in one-child households. They are popularly referred to as *xiao huangdi* or "little emperors," and their selfish ways are regularly deplored in China's state-run newspapers.

The one-child policy is more loosely enforced in the countryside, where farm families with as many as six children are not uncommon. But the only child is the urban norm, and these little emperors are a crucial market for companies establishing their brand presence in China. These kids are cosmopolitan and enthusiastic about trying new things, and have the disposable income to indulge their whims. Much as Generation Y is touted as the group for North American marketers to watch, China's little emperors are emerging as a driving force behind trends both within China and abroad, with an influence reaching as far as Europe and North America.

Coming of age amid the prosperity of China's booming cities, little emperors are better informed than any previous generation. Like their North American counterparts they are enthusiastic users of the latest consumer technology – portable DVD players, Internet-enabled cell phones – which they use to keep up with the latest in Tokyo fashions, Taiwanese pop music and Hollywood blockbusters. They love fast food from KFC, Pizza Hut and McDonald's, which contributes to North American-style weight problems: in big cities it's estimated that one in five children under 18 is obese.

The mindset of these new Chinese consumers is markedly different from that of people born in China before 1980. Under communism, people were taught to subordinate their individualism to the good of the collective. The new consumerist mindset teaches the reverse, and marketing experts advise companies entering the Chinese market to play to young people's desire for self-expression and create advertising messages emphasizing individuality, freedom and physical attraction. While older Chinese consumers shop for products that help them lead secure, orderly lives, those born since 1980 prioritize making a good impression on their peers and projecting their uniqueness.

Growing up in a market economy, China's young people are behaving just like young consumers in any other market economy. Now that technology provides them with easy access to current information on trends around the globe, they are joining their international contemporaries in the young person's eternal quest for status and peer acceptance through consumption. And new luxury goods are enormously important to these enthusiastic shoppers.

International chains are catering to this new market by expanding aggressively into China. Spanish fast-fashion retailer Mango, for example, had established itself in ten Chinese cities before opening its first North American stores in Toronto and Montreal in 2005. The power of the Chinese youth market will be increasingly embraced by international retailers, who will realize greater growth there than in the slower-growing, saturated markets of North America and Europe. Luxury brands will enjoy particular success, as Chinese youth's obsession with glittering Western lifestyles translates into larger markets for brand names associated with the good life.

We Are What We Buy

Purchasing luxury goods has taken on an almost religious significance for large numbers of consumers around the world. Freedom in the market democracy of the 21st century is widely interpreted as being able to buy as much as you can of whatever you want. Consumers of virtually any income level feel strongly that indulging their material whims is not a privilege, but a right.

In the United States and increasingly in other parts of the world, consumerism has beaten out political involvement and religion as the ideology that gives a sense of purpose and meaning to people's lives. Purchases have become consumers' primary means of projecting their personalities and reinventing themselves.

In his book *An All-Consuming Century: Why Commercialism Won in*

Modern America, historian Gary Cross writes that American life and the culture of consumption have become "so closely intertwined that it is difficult for Americans to see consumerism as an ideology or to consider any serious alternatives or modifications to it." According to Cross, consumers have unwittingly made a choice to define themselves and their communities through the ownership of goods.

If this truly is the belief system of the modern world, then shopping has become people's chief means of communicating who they are to their peers. Luxury goods like leather-upholstered SUVs and Burberry scarves are not only symbols of the good life, but extensions of the personalities of the people who buy them.

And when you are what you buy, you really ought to buy the best. As long as that still impresses your friends, of course.

Chapter 7

Discount Utopia

Experience vs. Commodity

THE last decade has seen a number of important changes in the consumer value equation. Rather than defining value in terms of price – that is, equating lower price with better value – consumers now tend to see value in terms of how the quality of the merchandise and the shopping experience relate to the price.

Today's consumers focus on total value, considering the retail experience in their value assessment. This trend has been developing for some time, and has been capitalized upon by retailers such as U.S. discounter Target, which offers great value combined with a treasure-hunt shopping experience.

Traditionally, retailers have relied on a commodity-based strategy that emphasizes price and assortment of merchandise. This has resulted in similar offerings and intense price competition. Several retailers have created in-house brands and have entered into exclusive agreements with suppliers, but these arrangements often fail to produce unique merchandise.

Retailers can escape the traps of the commodity-based strategy, however, by embracing an experience-based strategy. While still providing superior products, customers receive more value in-store through their shopping experience.

Competitors have more difficulty duplicating an experience-based strategy, which can focus on providing superior customer service, stimulating store environments, and even superior communities. On the other hand, not giving customers an exceptional in-store experience provides an opening for the competition to lure them away.

One of the paradoxes of modern retail is that many consumers expect features of what would have once been a high-end shopping experience even at low-end stores. By contrast, many affluent consumers are happy to shop at warehouse clubs and even dollar stores, as bargains and a treasure-hunt atmosphere have wide appeal. As a result, retailers have developed a variety of approaches to discounting, many of which are popular with consumers even in difficult economic times.

Welcome to Discount Utopia.

Value Means More than Lowest Price

People's expectations of retailers are higher than ever. Shoppers have little tolerance for long lines, out-of-stocks and sales staff who don't know the merchandise. They gravitate toward discounts, especially everyday low pricing.

At the same time, they expect high quality, great selection – in short, a "high value" shopping experience. Consumers want a range of choices, but can also be turned off by too much choice.

By creating clean, well-lit and well-designed shopping environments, value-oriented retailers like Target and many dollar store chains have turned their stores into good places to spend time browsing. If there was once a perceived social stigma to shopping at stores focused on the low end, it has largely evaporated as extreme-value shopping has become popular with people in a wide range of socio-economic groups.

Strategic Shopping

Today's consumer is, above all, well-informed. Now that the Internet is ubiquitous, pre-shopping has become the norm, and many consumers research even minor purchases extensively before entering a store.

Seasoned shoppers also rely on what they have learned about retail from years spent browsing stores and shopping centres. Department stores, in particular, have conditioned people to expect full price at the beginning of the season, followed eventually by clearance sales. Not only are savvy shoppers content to wait for the big sales, they have a sixth sense that tells them when desired items will be marked down to fire sale prices.

The strategic consumer will occasionally pay full-price, but only really enjoys opening her wallet for a discount. If a strategic consumer concludes an item she sees today will be marked down substantially tomorrow, she will wait to make the purchase.

Meanwhile, coupons available on shopping discount websites also allow bargain seekers to enjoy sale prices year-round.

In terms of shopping tactics, the shopper spectrum looks like this:

- **Myopic shoppers** – always purchase at the initial full price.
- **Bargain hunters** – only every purchase at a discount.
- **Strategic consumers** – buy at full price when necessary, but prefer to wait for a deal.

Since a significant proportion of customers shop strategically when given the chance, it makes sense for retailers to pay close attention to inventory levels. Lean inventory or "quick response" systems have been found to be considerably more profitable than the old sale-dependant model.

One retailer that has mastered the inventory game is Zara, whose business model limits discounts. The company stays on top of what sells and what doesn't, micro-managing inventory so each store's selection is kept fresh, and items that sell well are always on the shelves. This allows Zara to take advantage of quick turnaround on hot items, while offering little in the way of sales. Waiting for an item to be marked down at Zara doesn't typically pay off – shoppers who wait often find the item sold out.

Of course, not every retailer can successfully imitate Zara's quick response system, which depends on heavy investment in information technology and a variety of other tools (for more details, see the Zara section in Chapter 8). However, being prudent with inventory will help ensure success without frequent recourse to deep discounting.

In the future, retailers that stay on top of the trends and offer customers "less of more" – catering successfully to individual tastes as well as the broader consumer zeitgeist – will find it less necessary to offer the seasonal sales department stores have gotten us used to.

THREE KINDS OF BARGAINS

Consumers who want low-priced merchandise have a number of choices at their disposal: discount retailers, affordable store brands, and dollar stores. Here's the psychology that draws shoppers to each kind of bargain:

- **Discount retailers** sell name brands for less and appeal to consumers who see manufacturers' labels as a way of minimizing risk. These shoppers will forego conveniences and services to save money.
- **Retailers' brands** appeal to shoppers because they offer a good price point combined with acceptable quality. This represents good value for the money in the shopper's mind.
- **Dollar stores** and other low-price stores typically offer merchandise with relatively unfamiliar labels. Consumers may be willing to risk purchasing a low quality product in order to get the lowest price. Increasingly, these retailers offer brand name products – particularly secondary brands – to broaden their mainstream appeal.

Brand relevance varies greatly from one retail category to the next, and shoppers usually care much more about certain categories than they do about others. A shopper might look for her favourite fashion labels at a discounter, for example, and then buy cleaning supplies at a dollar store.

GENDER VALUES

A Wharton study entitled "Men Buy, Women Shop" makes a number of intriguing generalizations on the influence of gender on shopping habits. It suggests women shoppers do the bulk of what is normally termed "browsing," taking meandering trips through sprawling clothing collections with frequent detours through shoes and accessories. For men, on the other hand, shopping is a mission –most want to find what they came for and get out of the store as quickly as possible.

Women are said to react more strongly to interaction with sales associates, while men tend to focus on utilitarian concerns like parking, the length of the checkout line and whether the item they came for was in stock. The study found that for women, "lack of help when needed" was the top problem encountered while shopping (29%). The top challenge for men was difficulty finding parking close to a store's entrance (also 29%).

As for interactions with sales associates, men prized an associate's interest in helping them find an item, followed by the effort made to get them through checkout speedily. For women, it was more important that sales associates be familiar with the products in the store, and able to determine what best suits the customer. Women also appreciated sales people who make them feel important. The study suggests that, generally speaking, women want more interaction, and more collaboration and support in the buying process.

When retailers' operations are running smoothly and inconveniences like out-of-stocks and long checkout waits are at a minimum, there is the opportunity to add value to the shopping experience by segmenting customers, and segmenting by gender is an obvious approach. At the same time, there are plenty of men and women whose shopping habits do not reflect these broader patterns. Sales associates must always make an effort to tailor the service they deliver based on the shopping occasion, and above all on what the customer communicates.

TIGHTWADS VS. SPENDTHRIFTS

Another approach to segmenting consumers is by their spending habits. While some consumers scrimp and save, others spend lavishly through good times and bad.

Men tend to be bigger tightwads than women, while younger people tend to be bigger spendthrifts than older people. The more educated a person is, the more likely it is that he or she will be a tightwad.

Whether a person can be called a tightwad or a spendthrift depends on how much pain she feels when spending money:

- **Tightwads** are people who feel pain at the prospect of spending, and tend to spend less than they might like to.
- **Unconflicted consumers** experience moderate levels of pain while spending, and spend about what they want to spend.
- **Spendthrifts** find spending insufficiently painful, and tend to spend more than they would like to.

Tightwads are said to outnumber spendthrifts by a ratio of roughly three to two, according to a study by Wharton and Carnegie Mellon University. The good news for retailers is that determining which group customers fall into can be a useful tool in understanding who these customers are. Retailers can use techniques such as surveys and analysis of customer behaviour to help spell out which customers are spendthrifts and which are tightwads.

Approaches to spending differ most between the two groups with discretionary purchases like clothes or restaurant meals, whereas there is little difference in spending habits on "investment" purchases such as large appliances. In addition, the two groups enjoy a similar distribution of household income. Spendthrifts, however, are much more likely to carry large amounts of debt, while tightwads are more likely to have substantial savings.

As tightwads tend to be price-sensitive, stores might emphasize how painless it is to pay for a product with this group. Carefully choosing the language used in marketing communications – for instance, adding the word "small" to describe a fee – can help diminish a tightwad's resistance to spending. Spendthrifts, on the other hand, are more interested in the attributes of the products they buy, and prefer to hear about how much pleasure a purchase will bring them.

Marketers must keep in mind that ads and marketing communications often fail to speak to both groups. Ads stressing low price and savings speak directly to tightwads, while ads that focus on a product's attributes and how a product makes you feel resonate with spendthrifts. To find the right content and tone for marketing communications and customer service, marketers need to consider whether it's tightwads or spendthrifts they are trying to reach.

Shopping Experience Spectrum

These days the shopping spectrum breaks down into three main kinds of experience:

- Luxury
- Value
- Lowest price

Consumers tend to spend their dollars at either end of the spectrum, and there is strong growth for retailers offering the lowest price. That's because the ends of the spectrum give confused consumers the most clarity: at the upper end the consumer can be assured of quality, while at the low end the consumer is assured of a good price.

Retailers that built their business catering to the middle class, such as Sears, have found themselves squeezed in the last decade as consumers defected to either discounters or chains specialized in luxury goods. As I discuss in the Brand Obsession chapter, Starbucks' promise of a unique product and experience has to some extent been undermined by the ubiquity of its stores. When a retailer is perceived as serving everyone everywhere, consumers become less willing to pay a premium to shop there.

Consumers often see the middle of the spectrum as a compromise, even stress-inducing. When a retailer fails to clearly communicate a value message in a way that's easy to understand, consumers flee to retailers such as dollar stores, where the value message is refreshingly unambiguous.

The Value Proposition

Companies that try to be all things to all people end up exciting no one. On the other hand, a company that delivers exceptional levels of distinctive value to its target customers can achieve market leadership.

In terms of their value proposition, discounters and dollar stores trade on operational excellence. Price is front and centre, so they cultivate the consumer perception of offering the best deal. In addition, these retailers' operations are now so well-developed that the stores can succeed by trading on their value proposition alone.

There is a trend for discounters and dollar stores to increase their competitiveness in the area of product leadership by providing the "best" product or service. Many items exceed customers' minimum expectations of quality, shortening the list of items a customer would still be inclined to buy at traditional retailers.

More important, by increasing the number of name brand products they sell, dollar stores are reaching out to customers unwilling to gamble on product quality. This added reassurance greatly increases the category's appeal.

Price-Savvy Consumers

The growing popularity of retail chains focused on the low end can be attributed largely to consumers' voracious appetite for low prices, and the knowledge that these days acceptable quality can be had for very little.

Nonetheless, discount stores' appeal is still strongest among consumers of limited means. An AC-Nielsen survey indicated that U.S. shoppers with household incomes under $30,000 accounted for slightly more than half of dollar store sales. By comparison, the average Wal-Mart shopper is estimated to have a household income closer to $40,000, and that figure has risen as the retail giant's super centers attract affluent grocery shoppers.

Affluent shoppers are simultaneously becoming more at ease with the dollar store environment. More than in the past, people are unashamed of embracing retailers that provide items at lower price points than anyone else. In fact, the idea of guaranteed lowest prices, largely propagated by Wal-Mart, has become so engrained that many people believe a retailer is not doing its job if it is not delivering the lowest price.

Many traditional retailers have tried slashing prices to compete with discounters, but can only cut so deep into their already razor-thin margins. Consumers these days are savvy enough to recognize a significant discount, and patient enough to wait until they're convinced prices won't go any lower. At dollar stores, prices are rock-bottom all the time, which makes these retailers prime destinations for regular shopping trips.

Trading Up, Trading Down

In a world where even low-income individuals are habitual buyers of luxury goods, nine out of ten consumers frequent discount stores. What makes the low end so popular?

Today's debt-ridden consumer is always on the lookout for a bargain. More important, many consumers have lost sight of the advantages of dealing with full-service retailers. Shoppers have experienced poor customer service, including unattended cash registers, a lack of available sales staff and untrained staff unable to answer basic questions.

This doesn't mean these disgruntled consumers can't be lured back to full-service stores by retailers who deliver a satisfying full-service shopping experience. But customers shopping dollar stores and discounters are less demanding of store service, and the improved organization of these stores, combined with their straightforward displays and the uncomplicated nature of the items sold, result in a satisfying shopping experience for growing numbers of people.

A popular business mantra is "under-promise and over-deliver." Consumers have grown dissatisfied with department stores because they expect good service in these stores and are frequently disappointed. At discounters and dollar stores, consumers are more likely to expect a self-service environment. If sales associates are pleasant or knowledgeable, that's largely perceived as a bonus.

Where dollar stores and discounters are able to exceed customer expectation is in their merchandise selection. Customers are frequently amazed to find items that would cost them much more elsewhere. These stores are well-positioned to please customers, "over-delivering" on a regular basis.

The past decade has also seen a pronounced tendency for consumers to trade up in some categories while trading down in others. There are categories where people typically aim to save – cleaning supplies, for example – and where they seek out less expensive brands. Dollar stores are well-acquainted with these low-priority categories, stocking their shelves with items that fulfill price-sensitive needs.

In categories such as fashion, where people are more concerned about status, even middle-income consumers sometimes embrace the high end of the market and indulge in luxury brands. Yet discounters can benefit even when consumers develop extravagant spending habits. Saving money on day-to-day consumables and fashion basics suddenly becomes more important to an average-income consumer who has just bought a Louis-Vuitton bag.

Target: Discount Bull's-Eye

The year 1962 has a lot to answer for when it comes to discounting in America. Wal-Mart and Kmart launched that year, while the first Target store opened in Roseville, Minnesota. By 2008, Target was ranked 33rd in the *Fortune* 500, making it bigger than PepsiCo or Microsoft. The retailer continues to open about 100 stores a year.

In the past decade, the red and white circles of the Target logo have become as recognizable as the Nike swoosh, with an overwhelming 97% of Americans stating in a survey that they recognize the Target bull's-eye – in part thanks to the $1.2 billion the Minneapolis-based company spent on advertising in 2007. There are even Facebook groups devoted to discussing the retailer's many fine qualities.

Between 1998 and 2008, Target's revenues increased at about 12 per cent per year, to $63 billion. The stores' operating margins rose to 8.6 per cent, while those of Wal-Mart declined slightly to 7.3 per cent. Target hit a bump in the road at the end of 2007, when same-store sales dipped, causing the chain to miss earnings estimates. But while some analysts now criticize Target's strategies, its successes over the past decade qualify it as one of the most exciting discount concepts in retail today.

What distinguishes Target among discounters is the sometimes contradictory image summed up by its vision statement, "Expect more, pay less." The company was a leader in bringing high style to the discount arena, launching a line of affordably priced housewares designed by architect Michael Graves in 1999. These were followed by "mass/class" collections by designers including Philippe Starck and Todd Oldham.

The retailer's partnership with high-end fashion designer Isaac Mizrahi was also a hit, ending in 2008 after five successful years. Target's Go International collections, a program that aims to provide affordable fashions by world-renowned designers, began in 2006. Each guest-designed collection runs for up to 90 days; designers whose work is showcased have included Jovovich-Hawk, Gryson, Botkier, and Richard Chai. In 2008, Target announced it would keep the Go line going between guest-designed lines by selling fashions designed in-house.

Target's style savvy is enhanced by efforts to keep on top of global fashion trends, not unlike fast-fashion retailers H&M and Zara. Target's marketing department takes reports from the retailer's "creative cabinet," a team of a dozen people of all ages, interests and nationalities, who weigh in on matters such as the Go International collections or Target's slimmed-down cereal box with a self-locking top. By using its vast web of outside contacts, Target is able to make better decisions on what belongs in its stores.

One creative cabinet member, 80-year-old Liener Temerlin, is founder of agency Temerlin McClain. He made the invaluable suggestion that Target become founding sponsor of the AFI Dallas International Film Festival – a move that brings the retailer significant positive publicity in a key market. Clever marketing ideas like this help Target stand out in an ad-saturated world.

Innovation is a top priority for Target's 1,400-person marketing division. Bold new ideas are encouraged by requiring even established managers to bring exciting strategies to the table for their portion of the budget each year. In 2007, the concept for a holographic fashion show featuring virtual models won a significant piece of the marketing pie. Another winning idea was a vertical fashion show, where acrobats surprised onlookers by "walking" down the side of a building.

Target has escaped the kind of criticism levelled at Wal-Mart – in part because the company is only about one-sixth Wal-Mart's size – but the company is not universally admired. Some have pointed out the average pay provided by both Wal-Mart and Target in Minnesota (where Target is based) falls below $12.24 per hour, which advocacy group Jobs Now says is a living wage. No Target employees are unionized.

In addition, retail analysts have criticized the chain for inconsistent merchandising, which doesn't always live up to Target's impressive marketing. Studies have found consumers see Wal-Mart as a more affordable place to shop, even though Target's prices average out to within 1% to 3% of Wal-Mart's.

Yet Target maintains its special place in the discount universe by delivering a great shopping experience, and product that is exciting and unique. Innovation, design and quality, combined with the appeal of low prices, make Target customers some of the most enthusiastic discount shoppers around.

Stocking Up at Costco

Warehouse clubs, the original big box retailers, enjoy an enviable place in North American retail. These stores prosper even in challenging economic times, as a faltering economy encourages people to save by stocking up. The low unit prices that come with buying in bulk grow all the more appealing as consumers become more price-sensitive.

While I am not a great fan of the utilitarian shopping environments of warehouse clubs, one could argue these bare-bones environments enhance the sensation of saving money enjoyed by many club shoppers. Wal-Mart continues to install cheap linoleum and glaring fluorescent lighting at least in part because these environmental cues reinforce the retailer's low-price message.

The typical warehouse club also provides a dash of grandeur, with its soaring ceilings, vast selection and treasure-hunt atmosphere. Costco, in particular, has a reputation as a favourite destination for the affluent, thanks to a merchandise mix that includes everything from garbage bags to high-end diamond jewellery. At the same time, the palettes stacked with club packs reassure customers they are saving by shopping there.

Costco offers about 4,000 unique products for sale. On any given day, the retailer sells 103,000 rotisserie chickens – more than 37 million in the course of a year. But the biggest selling item at Costco is toilet paper, which accounts for $375 million in sales annually.

The high cost of gas also helps warehouse clubs thrive. Destination stores like Costco are among the few retailers in today's marketplace that can claim to offer true one-stop shopping, and consumers cutting down on long-distance shopping trips will still prioritize their preferred warehouse club. Stores that have their own gas stations are able to offer low prices at the pump, drawing consumers inside to shop for food and other consumables. In 2007, Costco sold 1.7 billion gallons of gasoline.

Warehouse clubs may see sales of luxuries like Swiss watches and trendy housewares slip during hard economic times, but they are better equipped than most retail categories to profit from a back-to-basics zeitgeist. Costco's winning value equation has made it the fourth-largest retailer in the U.S. – and yet it treats staff more generously than some of its low-price competitors.

ALMIGHTY DOLLARS

In the spring of 2008, journalist Henry Alford wrote an entertaining piece in the New York Times entitled "How to Survive in New York on 99 Cents." He details his forays into Manhattan's 99-cent stores, several of which offer constantly-changing assortments of bargain-priced delicacies.

After several weeks of sampling retailers' food lines, he prepares a gourmet meal entirely of 99-cent ingredients, and records the reactions of his friends to dishes such as chilled pear soup and flourless pecan torte. While the guests' praise is not necessarily glowing, Alford declares several of his penny-pinching recipes a success, and says he will continue to look for incredible value. "Bargain-hunting can be addictive," he writes.

Consumers increasingly crave the value and convenience that only dollar stores – also known as extreme-value retailers – can provide. The past decade has seen this once-lowly format move from retail's fringes into the mainstream. While mom & pop bargain emporiums remain, the dollar store of the 21st century is a well-merchandised cornucopia of great buys, increasingly giving competitors like traditional discounters a run for their money. Today's dollar store is seen by many enthusiastic shoppers as a convenient, time-saving alternative to big-box destinations like Wal-Mart. Dollar stores increasingly provide many of the other qualities shoppers demand in a shopping experience, such as cleanliness and attractive store environments.

The birth of the modern dollar store owes much to the economic downturn of the early '90s, when large numbers of consumers in North America and Japan developed a keen interest in discounted goods. Through the boom later that decade and subsequent economic uncertainty, dollar stores' popularity has continued to make gains. Ever-lower prices for goods imported from China, combined with the increasing social acceptance of discount formats, have earned a place for dollar stores among people's most-loved retail destinations, regardless of the state of the economy.

Wal-Mart responded to this rapidly growing threat by introducing dollar sections to certain U.S. stores. Target jumped into the dollar store frenzy by setting up a department called "The 1 Spot" in a number of its discount stores. Anxious for a piece of the Canadian action, Loblaw Cos. Ltd. introduced dollar-store aisles in some of its No Frills stores, while Great Atlantic & Pacific Tea Co. followed suit in some Food Basics locations.

More for Less

What's different about today's dollar store? Wider aisles, better lighting, tidier merchandising and better finishes set these stores apart from their cramped and cluttered ancestors. As a result, a broader range of shoppers have become dollar-store aficionados – from the bargain conscious to the affluent stocking up on party napkins and candles. Many better shopping centres have added a dollar store to round out their tenant mix.

While not all "dollar stores" sell items priced exclusively at one dollar, all deliver merchandise for prices generally under $10, and price points are disarmingly straightforward. Dollar General prices goods in round numbers ($1, $2, $3), while Canada's Dollarama prices everything at a dollar even.

The dollar-stores' merchandising tactics have grown sharper over the last decade, allowing them to sell items at a dollar that would have cost more than that at the wholesale level just a decade ago. The large chains import directly from overseas – mostly China – which eliminates the wholesaler and allows greater quality control. Dollar stores also keep costs down by buying merchandise at bargain basement prices from manufacturers that are unloading excess or end-of-the-line inventory.

It all adds up to a formula that delights shoppers, who know they would spend much more on the same item in a drugstore or a supermarket, or even a traditional discounter.

This is not to say dollar stores have no challenges of their own. Volume is key in the dollar-store business: the average dollar-store transaction is said to be less than $7 in Canada. And the format has not been immune to the challenging retail climate of the 21st century, as many locations have seen same-store sales level out or decline.

But as more North Americans discover the appeal of these bright new stores and their range of value-priced merchandise, the dollar store's role in fulfilling consumers' daily needs will continue to grow.

Competing with Retail's Giants

One of the most astonishing of the dollar stores' achievements is their ability to beat even Wal-Mart, the world's most efficient retailer, on price. They do so by maintaining ultra-low overheads and offering even fewer frills than Wal-Mart does.

Traditionally located in bleak strip malls and undesirable downtown pockets, dollar stores' locations keep real estate costs to a minimum. At the same time, the stores' small size allows them to set up in downtown neighbourhoods closer to where their customers live. Shoppers can complete their purchases in less time than it would take them to walk across a Wal-Mart parking lot.

Ironically, the rise of big-box discounters helped create the niche that dollar stores fill. Consumers who need to make a few quick purchases of everyday items may well balk at the idea of navigating the endless aisles of a big-box store. Dollar stores, on the other hand, are rarely larger than 10,000 square feet, making them easy for customers to find their way around.

Dollar General

By number of stores, Dollar General is the largest discount retailer in the U.S., with more than 8,200 locations in 35 states. Dollar General isn't strictly speaking a dollar store – many items are offered at higher price points. The retailer's slogan says much about its philosophy: "Save Time. Save Money. Every Day."

Early this decade, Dollar General made a substantial investment in technology and distribution, as well as testing an expanded grocery format. While experimenting with these new initiatives, the chain's business continued to grow, its revenue rising at double-digit rates. In fiscal 2007, same store sales grew at the healthy rate of 2.1 per cent, while smaller competitors such as Dollar Tree experienced a mild decrease. Dollar General had sales of $9.5 billion in fiscal 2007.

Dollar General's neighbourhood stores offers price-conscious customers over 5,000 branded items that fulfill daily needs, including food and snacks, health and beauty products, cleaning supplies, basic apparel, housewares and seasonal items. Food and other consumable basics account for about 60 per cent of Dollar General's sales. Brands carried by the retailer include Procter & Gamble, Unilever, Kellogg's, Nabisco and Fruit of the Loom.

Because low, even prices are the heart of Dollar General's business strategy, the retailer must negotiate with vendors to create sizes appropriate to its price points. While high-profile brands were at one time largely uninterested in supplying dollar stores with merchandise, many now produce special sizes for these retailers. Dollar General also leverages the power of national brands in its promotions, highlighting big names like Fruit of the Loom.

A sophisticated distribution system is indispensable to the success of any large retailer, and large dollar store chains take full advantage of new distribution technology. Dollar General's investment in an automated replenishment system and increased distribution capacity have aided its expansion across the U.S. Low prices alone cannot guarantee an extreme discount retailer's success; well-managed inventory and assortment are also crucial.

Dollar General has also experimented with a larger floor plate, its Dollar General Market concept. The new format is twice the size of a regular store, with a larger food selection including frozen and refrigerated foods and produce. A Freshness Guarantee is offered on all produce and meat, helping ensure consumers they are not sacrificing quality by buying food from a dollar store.

Dollar General's customers could be segmented into two main groups: those who are driven to extreme-value retailers out of necessity, and those who are less financially strapped but looking for a good deal. The retailer's strategy of stocking a comprehensive range of consumables and many top brands helps lure higher-income shoppers, who are delighted by Dollar General's low prices and small-store convenience.

DOLLARAMA

Canada's largest dollar store chain, Dollarama, was founded in 1992 by Larry Rossy, sometimes referred to as Canada's F.W. Woolworth. The retailer debuted as extreme-value shopping first appeared in Canada, gaining first-mover advantage. Its bright, attractively merchandised stores tend to be better organized than those of the competition, making them more appealing places to shop.

Over two million Canadians visit one of Dollarama's more than 500 locations each week. Dollarama's annual sales now total more than $1 billion, up from $508 million in 2003. The chain adds about 50 stores every year, expanding across Canada from its base in Ontario and Quebec. Private equity fund Bain Capital LLC of Boston acquired 80 per cent of the chain for a reported $1.03-billion in 2004, but it continues to be run by Mr. Rossy and his son Neil.

Dollarama has a big advantage over other discounters: although its shelves may be packed with a bewildering array of merchandise, there's no need to compare prices, because everything is priced at $1 (or, occasionally, two or three for $1). Uniform pricing speeds shopping up, because it relieves shoppers of the need to pause and deliberate over purchases. There's generally no need to choose between the reasonably-priced store brand and the name brand on special, as there would be in a traditional store environment. The simplicity of the dollar store environment saves consumers valuable time, as well as money.

Dollarama has another important competitive advantage in Rossy's shrewd buying practices. The retailer's size allows for economies of scale and direct sourcing from China, helping to keep prices attractive. Dollarama has developed about 70 house brands; unlike Dollar General in the U.S., the retailer does not rely on the appeal of national brands to draw in shoppers. Like its American cousin, Dollarama offers about 5,000 products.

Discount real estate is another important part of the Dollarama equation. Low-rent locations such as basements are sought out by the chain, in order to compensate for the stores' $210-per-square-foot average sales. In addition, Rossy rejected the idea of franchising, and all the stores are corporately owned. Landlords love Dollarama, since the stores work in moribund strip malls as well as high-end shopping centres. At 9,000 to 10,000 square feet, they are over twice the size of typical dollar stores, making them shopping destinations in their own right.

According to Rossy, Dollarama specializes in categories where consumers don't want to spend a lot, and quality can be "just good enough." The stores stock many items that appear to be worth more than $1, such as desk-size calculators and "industrial quality" tools, ensuring consumer enthusiasm and encouraging impulse purchasing.

Like most dollar store chains, Dollarama emphasizes holiday and seasonal merchandise, which helps keep the shopping experience exciting year-round. Halloween, Christmas and Valentine's Day provide occasions for remerchandising the front of each store with fast-moving cards, decorations and costumes. Winter hats and gloves are offered in the fall, while garden tools appear in the early spring.

Dollarama employs a variety of low-tech practices to keep costs in check. The retailer accepts no credit card payments, just cash and debit. All items cost $1, eliminating time-consuming price-tagging, and there are no scanners at checkouts. Store staff must count inventory and feed the information into a computer to determine which items are being over- or under-stocked. Rising commodity prices may present a challenge to maintaining the $1 price point for some items, but the retailer will adjust its offering where necessary – for instance, by putting nine erasers in a package instead of twelve.

Larry Rossy estimates there is one dollar store per 32,000 Canadians, compared to one per 12,000 in the U.S. As a result he places no ceiling on the chain's potential for growth. Its one significant rival, Buck Or Two, shrank to 141 stores after its master franchisor filed for creditor protection in 2004. There's no doubt Dollarama's ongoing expansion is a welcome development for affluent and price-sensitive consumers alike.

DAISO: STYLE FOR $2

A hundred Japanese Yen is roughly equivalent to two Canadian dollars – so when Japanese mega-chain Daiso opened its first North American location in suburban Vancouver in 2003, everything in the store was priced at $2. All the products the retailer sells are specifically made for Daiso, including an enticing array of food items, cosmetics, fabric flowers, storage containers, stationery, gift wrap and traditional Japanese ceramics.

First incorporated in 1977, Daiso is the number one value retail chain in Japan, opening about twenty new stores every month in its domestic market. Daiso now has over 2,500 stores in Japan, and an additional 470 worldwide. Since 2001, the retailer has added locations in countries including Korea, Singapore, Romania, Saudi Arabia, New Zealand and the U.S.

Daiso's Canadian pilot store at the ultra-modern Aberdeen Centre in Richmond, British Columbia, has enjoyed considerable success. Like Toronto's Pacific Mall, the 380,000-square-foot shopping centre was built to cater to the needs of the region's Asian inhabitants, who account for the majority of the population in this Vancouver suburb. Consequently, Daiso benefited from high brand recognition from the start. By all accounts it is one of Aberdeen Centre's most popular retailers, breaking all of Daiso's previous sales and traffic records for opening stores.

The two-floor Richmond location, at nearly 30,000 square feet, has been likened to Ikea in its design sensibility. About 50,000 different items are on offer, with 700 new items appearing on the shelves each month to maintain a high level of customer excitement. The store has been lauded for its attractive, tidy displays, which give it the atmosphere of a department store despite the low price point.

A deal made between Daiso-Sangyo Co. of Japan and Thomas Fung, chief executive of privately-held Fairchild Property Group Ltd., was responsible for bringing the retailer to Canada. Fung negotiated with major North American shopping centre owners to establish more Daiso locations, opening nine stores in the U.S. by 2008.

Critics, however, say Daiso's offering is not significantly different from that of the dollar store chains already familiar to North Americans, and no Canadian stores have been opened since the Richmond pilot location. It could be that

Central Canada is perceived as inhospitable to new extreme-value retailers, thanks to Dollarama's hold on the market.

The Future of Value

This decade's shopper demands a great deal from her shopping experience. Low everyday prices, speedy transactions and the excitement of a treasure hunt are all elements that draw consumers to shop one store over another.

U.S. retailers Costco and Target have developed unique strategies that appeal to the desire for value in a wide range of consumers. Costco's selection and shopping experience are made more appealing by the retailer's gas bars, while Target has leveraged people's increasing desire for style in its innovative marketing and reasonably-priced designer goods. Dollar stores, meanwhile, are positioned to take advantage of a niche created by big-box discounters, using advances in supply chain technology and importing directly from overseas to deliver extreme-value shopping on a convenient scale.

As a result, traditional retailers are being forced to re-examine their strategies and find ways to convince shoppers that extreme value is not the only kind of value. Few consumers can resist the feeling of satisfaction you get from a great deal.

CHAPTER 8

BRAND OBSESSION

WHY BRANDS MATTER

STRONG brands evoke satisfying experiences. If a brand provides satisfaction and makes someone happy to part with her money, it has done much to cultivate the loyalty marketers aim for. In the retail world, a brand's strength is built on the combined experience of thousands of customers.

Unfortunately, some companies believe hype and hype alone will convince consumers their branded goods and services are better than what the competition offers. Though this approach can enrich corporations and their shareholders in the short term, making promises a brand cannot live up to results in dissatisfied, disillusioned customers. Only brands that offer lasting value cultivate loyalty.

In an era when many products and services seem interchangeable, branding is one of the few things that can help consumers distinguish between products that are otherwise identical in terms of quality, reliability or price. Branding is supposed to help forge a relationship between consumer and brand, often creating aspirational lifestyles that people can take part in by buying the brand.

A brand's real value, however, is its ability to please and persuade consumers. Skilled brand managers understand it is not always the best product or service, technically speaking, that wins consumers over. Success depends on how well a brand reflects what target consumers want, and how they perceive value. Preferred brands can be relied on to provide specific consumers with specific satisfying experiences.

In a world where consumers hold increasing power over manufacturers and retailers, brands need to work harder to provide more genuine gratification to satisfy and surpass expectations. Informed consumers will shun brands that fail to live up to the hype surrounding them, thanks to the speed at which word travels via the Internet.

Brand and Value

Focused and effective brand management is crucial to business survival. While brand can by no means be applied in every situation, branding and its associated benefits can provide an invaluable competitive advantage in an increasingly crowded and changeable marketplace.

A brand must clearly and consistently communicate its unique value proposition while striving for differentiation. A strong brand name evokes a perception of added value for which consumers may be willing to pay a premium. Increasingly in the retail world, strong brands connote "value" in the sense of good quality at lower prices.

The Retail Brand

For retailers and shopping centres, a brand is a promise conveyed to customers by everything they can observe:

- Service (the way the brand's representatives treat customers)
- Price points
- Shopping environment
- Signage
- Displays
- The brand name and logo
- Advertising and Web presence

Strong brands harmonize all of these points so customers know what to expect when they walk into a store, and look forward to returning.

Progressive retailers work hard to deliver more than customers expect. At Ikea, for example, prices of certain items have fallen over time instead of going up, thanks to the chain's ongoing efforts to improve efficiency. Home décor lines are also frequently refreshed. Customers visiting Ikea find themselves thinking, "It was good before, but now it's even better." This is exactly the kind of impression every retailer's brand should try to evoke.

Cult Brands

Brands often communicate concepts such as prestige, convenience or durability. But leading brands emphasize a message of belonging, creating a following and breeding intense loyalty.

Almost half of Harley-Davidson owners, for instance, have previously owned a Harley. The legendary motorbike maker is an excellent example of the kind of brand so popular with a core group of enthusiasts that it achieves cult status.

A cult brand generally starts out small and builds its following gradually, sometimes over a period of several years. Harley- Davidson, founded in 1903, only took off in the '40s as returning World War II veterans took to the road on the powerful bikes.

Extreme groups of consumers sometimes display their affection for cult brands in unnerving ways. For example, thousands of Apple computer fans attend San Francisco's annual MacWorld expo with religious zeal. Manolo Blahnik shoes, some of which go for over US$3,000 a pair, are nothing short of addictive. Urban myths abound about customers acquiring more than 100 pairs.

Imaginative marketing may help a brand attract an intensely loyal following, but advertising that fails to resonate with the product's core customers can also drive people away. Businesses that maintain their authenticity while attracting a growing group of customers, like Harley Davidson, are making excellent use of their brand. They continue to deliver on the brand's promise, to both new customers and those already enjoying the feeling of belonging that has become an integral part of the brand.

The Savvy Customer

Companies must be at the top of their game to succeed in retail today. I have reiterated this point in every chapter because the customer has never been more in control. And customers demand the same best practices from all industries, as they no longer distinguish based on the product or service.

This is why banks, for example, increasingly behave like retail boutiques, in an effort to meet the consumer desire for a satisfying experience.

Sales performance is largely a function of matching an offering to the most appropriate customer. Brands are extremely valuable in communicating attributes and benefits to the right audience, and can make a strong case for the ongoing relevance of the product or service. Customization also plays a role, as technology enables customers to enjoy both products and transactions – by phone or via an e-commerce website, for instance – custom-tailored to their desires.

Apple initially tailored its offering to a key segment of the personal computer market, making itself so relevant to that group of consumers that it could not be displaced by a competitor. The company's success as gadget maker to the masses was built upon this strong branding. A strong brand has helped Apple maintain its aspirational air of cool, even as its products have become ubiquitous.

Brand Management and Business Growth

In order to thrive, a brand needs to grow organically, rather than merely growing by acquisition. A strong brand is its own best ambassador when it enters new markets, creating product or line extensions, or seeking out alliances and co-branding partners.

Consumers must perceive the brand's extensions as credible, however. Crest and Colgate continue to expand their offerings of types of toothpaste, teeth whiteners, dental floss, and electric toothbrushes because customers have given the companies the right to produce these additional products. People see these products as appropriate extensions for brands synonymous with toothpaste.

A strong brand acts as an effective lever for measured and appropriate organic growth. Brands play a significant role in the search for new revenue streams, and the stream most readily tapped into is licensing. Appropriate brand extensions can prove lucrative. On the other hand, a company that licenses its brand too prolifically may face quality issues, negatively impacting the equity of the original offering.

A case in point is the licensing of the Caterpillar brand into apparel, footwear and accessories. The successful manufacturer of backhoes and forklifts licensed its brand to Wolverine World Wide in 1994, and the footwear manufacturer began making the now-famous Caterpillar boots and shoes. Thanks in part to a reputation for quality that reflects the machine maker's brand promise, Caterpillar footwear is now marketed in over 120 countries on six continents. A full range of apparel and accessories further leverages the brand's reputation for quality.

Inspiring Employees

The benefits of a strong brand go beyond finding and keeping customers. Staff can be inspired by a brand's strengths to bring more of their energy and enthusiasm to the retail workplace, while job seekers often apply first to businesses whose brands have positive associations.

A strong brand provides invaluable aid in the search for talent, because potential employees evaluate brands and the companies they represent in much the same way consumers do. Companies are embracing the concept of internal brand alignment to attract and retain the best employees and enhance productivity. A strong brand saves on recruiting time, and helps ensure the employee's relationship with the company has a solid foundation.

Internal branding is an increasingly important focus. While employees were once the last to hear about the latest marketing communications campaign, now many companies begin by educating employees on new marketing messages and initiatives. This approach helps align customer service with the company's brand, ensuring marketing promises are delivered. In great companies, brand is a central organizing principle that plays a role in all decision making.

Brand Equity: Attracting and Keeping Customers

There are four levels of brand awareness that need to be considered in the process of building a brand:

Attributes. These are usually descriptive phrases that, through promotion, get attached to a product. "Enjoy Coca-Cola," "Always fresh."

Benefits. The attributes must provide functional benefits. Volvo's advertising messages typically focus on crash-worthiness, so Volvo drivers buy safety as part of the car's benefit package.

Values. That is, the lifestyle values of the consumer. People buy Rolex watches because, besides being excellent timepieces, they say something about the buyer's self-image.

Personality. Brands reflect personality. People tend to choose products that match their perceptions of their own personalities. Harley-Davidson reflects a personality different from the personality you'd associate with a BMW touring bike.

THE ROLE OF PRICE

Although brand has an enormous influence on how much consumers are willing to pay for a product or service, businesses are often unable to predict how consumers will react to the prices they set. Research has shown repeatedly that consumers do not have an accurate idea of how much most products cost.

In a world of abundant purchase options, shoppers may know items' relative prices – branded Kellogg's Cornflakes cost more than No Name cornflakes, for example. But they are unlikely to know the exact price of a 42" Panasonic LCD television at a given store, or whether an equivalent TV by Toshiba will be more or less expensive.

Though consumers often don't know the exact price of the items they buy, their knowledge of products' relative value allows them to produce an estimate of what a given item should cost. For example:

A customer might believe a basic cup of coffee ranges in price from 50 cents to $3, with the average cup costing $1.50.

The customer knows the Starbucks coffee is near the top of the range, and estimates it will cost $3.

If the customer orders a coffee at Starbucks and it costs her $5, she will therefore find the coffee expensive.

When the customer finds out the coffee costs $1.98, she is pleasantly surprised – even though the price is easily more than twice the cost of the same item at McDonald's.

To understand shoppers' views of the relationship between brand and pricing, businesses need to consider how they assign price estimates based on the category the item belongs to. Starbucks, for example, sells premium specialty coffees, while McDonald's does not. This is why Starbucks can charge more.

What does this mean for retailers? When a price is above what the consumer estimates it should be for a given item in a given category, the consumer will demand a decrease, or simply wait for the item to go on sale. A price that's slightly below the customer's estimate, on the other hand, will create the perception of good value.

Retailers like Wal-Mart, Zara and Ikea, which consistently offer items priced below customers' expectations, have built a thriving business on delivering what is widely seen as "good value."

Branding Opportunities

Brands need to cultivate the following qualities:

Memorability
Making a brand interesting makes it memorable.

Credibility
A company steeped in expertise inspires confidence.

Trust
Customers perceive a trustworthy brand as dependable, honest and sensitive to consumer needs.

Community
Contributing to the community enhances the brand by making it liked. Consumers more readily accept a liked brand's message.

Quality
Quality can be communicated by showing the product is superior to that of competitors.

Symbolism
Consumers remember a product better when they can associate it with a strong symbol.

Meaning

A strong brand identity can create a sense of pride, purpose and meaning that inspires customers and motivates employees.

Loyalty

Building a brand helps develop customer loyalty, enhancing the brand's ability to attract and keep customers.

Value

Enhancing the brand strengthens its value proposition. This includes emotional and self-expressive benefits, as well as functional benefits.

Experience

Creating the brand means building an aspirational shopping centre or store environment, as well as an aspirational shopping or product experience.

During the past decade, I have been particularly impressed by three dynamic and distinct retailers that have come to personify the ultimate in branding. Starbucks, Zara and Ikea have taken all of the above points into consideration in building their brands. Strong branding, communicated at every point of contact with customers, is at the root of their worldwide success.

STARBUCKS: FROM MASS TO CLASS TO MASS

There are plenty of places to buy a cup of coffee. Most of them – 7-Eleven, Tim Hortons and McDonald's, for instance – offer the beverage for considerably less than Starbucks. How does Starbucks manage to charge $2, $3 or $4 for a kind of drink that used to cost 50 cents? And how did Starbucks grow to become one of the world's most recognizable brands in a couple of decades?

Despite the undeniable strengths of the Starbucks branding formula, it's important to point out that the chain is no longer enjoying the spectacular success it enjoyed in the '90s and early 2000s. In 2008, the company recorded its first-ever declines in U.S. comparable store sales and transactions. For one thing, harsh economic realities are prompting U.S. consumers to spend less.

Nonetheless, Starbucks' global popularity remains one of the outstanding achievements in modern branding. Let's examine the phenomenal success enjoyed by this universally known brand.

The Starbucks Story

Starbucks as we know it was conceived in 1983, when Chairman Howard Schultz paid a visit to Milan. He had been working as Director of Retail Operations and Marketing for the small Seattle-based company – at that time a purveyor of coffee beans, not beverages – for about a year. It struck him that it was the right moment to import Italian espresso bar culture to the U.S.

Starbucks' owners weren't willing to try the concept, so Schultz opened his own small chain of espresso bars, Il Giornale, in Vancouver and Seattle. A couple of years later, Starbucks' owners were ready to sell, so Schultz raised the $3.8 million to buy the chain. By 2008, Starbucks had more than 15,000 stores in 42 countries.

A Cup of Lifestyle

What exactly are you paying for when you walk through Starbucks' doors and plunk down $4 for a caramel macchiato?

Atmosphere, for one thing. Starbucks' carefully calculated ambiance is intended to complement the modern lifestyle. Cozy couches and listenable music make the neighbourhood Starbucks ideal for working on a laptop, reading or holding a small meeting. It's also a place to buy gifts and gift cards.

Starbucks has made café culture such a significant part of North American life that for many the chain has become, to borrow a favourite phrase of Howard Schultz's, their "third place" – where they spend the most time, after home and work.

Pour Me Another

The chain's breakneck expansion and skyrocketing revenues – which rose by about 20 per cent annually, year after year– reflected that consumers were willing to embrace Schultz's dream in ever-larger numbers.

One might expect that the chain's substantial profits come from the high cost of its specialty beverages. Indeed, over three-quarters of the company's retail business is generated by the beverages it sells.

Of every retail dollar spent at Starbucks

- 40 cents covers store-level operating expenses

- 50 cents pays for the cost of sales and occupancy expenses
- 10 cents trickles down as profit (6 or 7 cents after taxes).

The cash flow generated by this formula is what funds Starbucks' expansion. The company has next to zero long-term debt, and doesn't rely on selling stock to build new stores.

Starbucks distinguishes itself from old guard fast food chains like McDonald's by not franchising, which Schultz insists would mean a loss of control over his stores.

In an effort to reach more consumers more of the time, some stores are kept open 24 hours. Specialty drinks like teas and Frappucinos were invented to maintain customer interest year-round.

The introduction of automatic espresso machines made service faster than ever. Some industry observers, however, view this innovation as a misstep. How exclusive is a beverage made by a machine?

Starbucks has also been celebrated for the way it treats staff. Employees who work more than 20 hours a week receive health-care benefits and stock options. For Schultz, employees who have stock in the company are likely to care more about their customers. It's a fact that this kind of thinking continues to generate enthusiasm among Starbucks employees, and helps steer Starbucks clear of the employee relations troubles that can bedevil less generous employers.

A Strong Cup of Branding

Outside the realm of technology, Starbucks is easily one of the strongest retail brands conceived in the last two decades of the twentieth century. The company leverages that strength through brand extensions:

- Starbucks sells ready-to-drink coffee beverages, along with several flavours of coffee ice cream.
- Schultz bought Starbucks its own record label in 1999, which has since released over a hundred albums and sold millions of CDs. In 2007, Paul McCartney put out his album *Memory Almost Full* on Starbucks' new Hear Music label.
- The company teamed up with Bank One to offer the Starbucks

> Card Duetto Visa, a traditional credit card and a stored-value card combined, which gives customers Starbucks points for using the Visa.

This is not to say all of Howard Schultz's efforts to extend the brand have succeeded. Starbucks' 1999 experiment in publishing, a magazine called *Joe* rolled out with Time Inc., was a notorious flop.

New Luxury or Old News?

In its first two decades, Starbucks' winning philosophy was based on a sound understanding of North American consumers and their desire to trade up. By making what was once a humdrum beverage into an aspirational item, Starbucks forever altered the way we think about coffee. The company's branded drinks, beans and gifts became "new luxury" items, appealing to people's longing for the good life at relatively modest prices.

But these days there is more competition in the premium coffee arena. McDonald's has entered the barista business, with plans to install coffee bars at its 14,000 U.S. stores. The fast food chain uses theatrics similar to Starbucks', displaying espresso machines, serving biscotti and having baristas prepare drinks. Starbucks transformed coffee from a commodity into an experience, but McDonald's is now set to turn it back into a commodity.

In addition, Starbucks has forfeited its air of exclusivity by making itself available everywhere. Those who want a truly premium cup of joe have a variety of smaller, upscale cafés to choose from, while those who prefer to spend less have no shortage of $1-a-cup options. This leaves Starbucks, once associated with luxury, in the ill-defined middle ground that has proved so problematic for traditional department stores like Sears.

Finally, rampant overexpansion has caused the chain to cannibalize its own business. As a result, Starbucks is closing underperforming U.S. and Australian stores, and scaling back new-store openings.

In the early days, Starbucks encouraged customers to treat coffee as one would wine, with the keen nose and taste buds of the connoisseur. As it became a mass purveyor of standardized beverages, the company subverted its own brand promise.

Initially, going to Starbucks and paying $4 for a coffee meant you were separating yourself from the mainstream. Strolling along a city street with a

Starbucks cup in hand became an affirmation of class. But for an item to have elevated class associations, it must remain somewhat scarce, which Starbucks has long since ceased to be. By adopting a program of supercharged growth, the company abandoned its claim to exclusivity. This chain of events has seen Starbucks' share price drop more than 50 per cent from its peak.

Today's coffee connoisseur seeks a more authentic specialty coffee experience, while many average consumers are disenchanted with the kind of corporate expansion Starbucks is seen to represent. Smaller, hipper shops and chains, benefiting from Internet-enabled buzz, are now the go-to coffee shops for the image-conscious.

Is it possible to become a global phenomenon without compromising your brand? The success of both Zara and Ikea suggest it is. And despite its recent challenges, Starbucks can still be held up as a model of global branding success. Solid brand principles go a long way toward ensuring a retail brand's longevity.

ZARA: FAST FASHION ICON

The company that redefined global fashion is neither a Paris couture house nor a hip London design emporium, but rather a retailer in La Coruña, Spain, which gets affordable fashions to market in the blink of an eye. This formula helped its parent company, Inditex, grow by 25 per cent a year and open more than 1,100 Zara stores in 68 countries by 2008. Launched in 2002, Zara Home has also proved an international success, with over 200 stores. And all this has been achieved without advertising. How does Zara do it?

Live Collections

Started in the '70s by reclusive Spaniard Amancio Ortega, Spain's richest man, Zara is arguably the world's most innovative fashion retailer. It ships new products to its stores weekly, not once a season. Its stores stock more than 11,000 products. In the past decade the chain's steady and carefully calculated expansion has brought its fashions to enthusiastic customers in markets as far flung as Morocco, Lithuania, Oman, Panama and Indonesia.

The key to the company's success lies in its "live collections." Up-to-the-minute styles are made available to eager shoppers with blinding speed. On average, the company takes just ten to fifteen days from sketching a new design to delivering the piece of clothing to its stores.

Like its competitors, Zara understands people have come to view fashion as a disposable commodity. Zara, however, takes a third of the time of H&M or Gap to get new styles into the hands of consumers. Its competitive advantage is rooted largely in its superb use of technology and astonishingly efficient and responsive manufacturing and distribution.

Zara's products are stylish and aspirational, but priced low enough that items are mostly guaranteed not to be in the shop for long. Many fashion-hungry consumers have abandoned the "investment" approach to clothes shopping represented by well-established luxury brands such as Prada. Instead, people are opting for the democratic pleasure of style so affordable it does not need to be worn for more than a season to justify its cost.

Through its Zara Home concept, the retailer applies a similar approach to home fashions, offering affordable goods that allow customers to feather their nests in style.

Getting the Styles to the Stores

Unlike many apparel manufacturers, Zara doesn't rely on cheap labour in developing countries to keep prices low. Although some basic items like T-shirts and jeans, which account for 20 per cent of Zara's selection, are imported from Asia, much of the retailer's stock is still manufactured at a sprawling and highly automated complex in La Coruña.

The five-level distribution centre stretches almost half a million square metres. Garments travel from the adjoining manufacturing plants along 200 kilometres of underground tracks. Optical devices read their electronic tags, sorting and distributing more than 60,000 items of clothing every hour. Twice a week a fleet of trucks leaves La Coruña laden with items destined for stores around the world.

The company keeps on top of the latest fashion trends by sending staff to university campuses, nightclubs and other havens of the hip to observe what the young and fashion-obsessed are wearing. Every day, headquarters gathers data from four continents on late-breaking trends.

At the store level, customers provide feedback on the garments and colours they'd like to see on the racks. Zara's manufacturing apparatus is so responsive that if an item isn't selling, it can be re-dyed in a different range of colours. Zara minimizes the risk of stocking an unpopular style by producing in small batches, avoiding overstocking, and scrapping the production of anything that doesn't sell. New fashion lines are routinely created in days.

Zara has only two sales a year, since the vast majority of its output can be sold at full price. Very little gets remaindered.

The retailer also distinguishes itself from less fashion-oriented companies by setting up in prime locations. Zara builds nearly identical storefronts in cities around the world, from Paris to Beirut to Singapore to Toronto. The sophisticated ambiance of its stores reinforces the message that customers should be able to enjoy both the shopping experience and the fashions at less than high-fashion prices.

Zara Home

Zara's clothing stores account for most of the income of its parent company, Spanish group Industria de Diseno Textil, or Inditex. In addition to expanding its other retail chains, including Massimo Dutti and Bershka, it rolled out its Zara Home concept in 20 stores in Spain and Portugal beginning in August 2002.

After its first five years of operation, Zara Home had 200-plus stores across Europe. Its first location in the English-speaking world was across from Harrod's in Knightsbridge, London.

Zara Home offers a variety of rustic and ethnic-inspired made-in-Spain items that reflect the latest trends in home fashion and design. The concept adheres to the formula that has made Zara's clothing lines so successful, constantly updating the offering. Products include textile items for bed, table and bath, plus small household and décor items, as well as a home spa collection.

The Zara Home catalogue presents a highly sophisticated image, with gorgeous full-page colour photographs evoking a lush mood. The website uses the same rich visuals, and helps customers find stores via an interactive map of Europe. The site also pitches the company's gift cards.

Critics of Zara's expansion, especially in North America, say the chain's Spain-centred network faces challenges in terms of international distribution. Indeed, North American shoppers may well find Zara clothes less of a bargain than European customers, because pricing reflects the cost of distribution.

The high Euro also presents its challenges to keeping North American prices affordable.

And Zara Home, with its mirrors, glassware and other fragile items, will require its own purpose-built distribution system as the chain grows. To become a truly global brand, Zara will need to reproduce its European distribution system on other continents. Meanwhile, this innovative Spanish retailer continues to transform the apparel and home fashion markets with its affordable, desirable styles.

Ikea: Home Décor Redefined

From its humble origins in the town of Almhult, Sweden, Ikea has become the world's most powerful furniture retailer. Its brand has become synonymous with stylish home décor at rock-bottom prices.

The company's corporate mantra is "Low price with meaning." That is, Ikea aims to make merchandise less expensive without making customers feel cheap. The success of the Swedish powerhouse is rooted in its ability to provide good quality and contemporary style at price points that generally beat the competition's prices by 30 to 50 per cent. Innovation and astonishing efficiency characterize Ikea's design, manufacturing, shipping and retailing practices, ensuring that customers who visit an Ikea store are rarely disappointed.

Ikea was started in 1943 by 17-year-old Ingvar Kamprad (the name is made up of his initials plus the first letters of the names of his family's farm and village), and by 2008 it had 273 stores in 37 countries, with some 583 million customers each year. Midway through the first decade of the new millennium, sales exceeded US$1-billion per month. Worldwide, year-over-year sales growth regularly exceeds 20 per cent.

Ikea has created its own unique niche in the retail market, and the brand has positive connotations for an ever-larger group of consumers around the globe.

Putting Price First

Manufacturers of furniture and home décor items usually start with a design and find an economical way to produce it, but Ikea starts with the price point, then sets out to make the item for the target price.

There are four basic styles: young Swede (bare bones), modern (minimalist), country (neo-traditional), and Scandinavian (sleek wood). These are sold in three basic price ranges: low, medium and high. Product managers lay out items on a graph (a "price matrix") to determine what's available at a given price point. New items are commissioned where there are holes in the product lineup.

If, for example, a product manager discovers he has no stand-alone kitchen islands in the low price range, he will set out to fill the gap by surveying similar offerings from competitors and establishing a price point 30 to 50 per cent lower than theirs. Before the product is even designed, Ikea will determine what materials it will be made of, and find a manufacturer among its 1,800 suppliers in 55 countries who can produce it in sufficient quantities at the target price point.

Once a manufacturer has been found, the product manager writes up a brief outlining the product's price and function, the fabricator's capabilities and the materials to be used. The brief is sent to Ikea's pool of staff designers and freelancers. Promising designs are refined, and the product manager selects the one that will eventually appear on store shelves.

Ikea also gives each item a Swedish-sounding nickname, and attaches designers' names to the products in catalogues and on the website. These strategies enhance the notion that Ikea products have more personality than anonymous products from other manufacturers. Using the designer' names highlights the fact that Ikea's design benefit from a sophisticated Scandinavian sensibility.

Not unlike Zara, Ikea has a "product strategy council." This group of senior executives follows consumer trends around the globe and makes appropriate changes to the product lineup, ensuring Ikea stays ahead of changes in the way people furnish and decorate their homes.

Savings at Every Step

Ikea customers don't seem to mind the fact that so much of the store's merchandise needs to be assembled. That's a good thing, because shipping disassembled items in flat boxes is one of the keys to Ikea's low prices.

In fact, shipping items flat is an Ikea invention. One day in 1956, an Ikea designer watched a customer trying to cram a table into his car, and had the idea that selling disassembled items in boxes would largely solve the problem. Since then, most of the retailer's products have been designed to be taken apart so they slide easily into a station wagon or onto a roof rack. This approach saves the company vast amounts on shipping: Ikea estimates transport volume would increase six times if it shipped items assembled, and the retail cost of its products would rise 25 per cent.

The importance of saving space in shipping containers influences the design of even small products. The Bang mug, for instance, has been redesigned three times. Originally, only 864 mugs would fit on a pallet. Adding a rim like the one you'd see on a flowerpot made it possible to fit 1,280 mugs onto a pallet. In its third incarnation, the mug was shortened and fitted with a new handle, so a pallet now holds 2,024 of them. While the price of the mug has stayed the same, shipping costs have been reduced 60 per cent, and the cost of production at Ikea's Romanian factory has fallen because the mugs take up less space in the kiln.

As more of Ikea's products are manufactured in the Far East – China has replaced Sweden as the country supplying the largest portion of merchandise – reducing the cost of shipping becomes increasingly important. In addition to making its goods ship in the smallest amount of space possible, the retailer has created a global network of 18 distribution centres, most near major container ports, railways and truck routes. These handle about 70 per cent of Ikea's product line, while the other 30 per cent travels directly from supplier to store.

Sometimes the components of a given product are not reunited until they reach the store. A chair frame may be manufactured in Poland (one of the company's chief manufacturing countries), while the cushion comes from China.

Trend-Conscious Design

Part of Ikea's success stems from its relevance to the modern lifestyle. The company's philosophy may be rooted in the uncomplicated ways of rural Sweden, but the up-to-date merchandise mix reflects a keen knowledge of the current needs of consumers all over the world.

Ikea's abundant design solutions for people living in small spaces reflect the widespread trend toward smaller households. The impressive selection of both sleek and homey office furniture acknowledges the increasing popularity of home offices. New product lines consistently reflect popular home décor trends.

Ikea is also in step with parents who feel their kids deserve cool-looking bedrooms, and the retailer knows kids with divorced parents often have a bedroom at both parents' homes. That's why Ikea carries an abundance of décor items targeted at kids, such as colourful lamps, toys, furniture and storage solutions.

Young families, traditionally among the retailer's best customers, find their baby needs well looked after. There are highchairs, cribs, plates and cutlery for the under-two set. Ikea also makes use of marketing initiatives aimed at kids, such as a kids' bedroom design contest it held to help entice tween buyers.

Indulgent pet owners find a wide range of items designed to help them accommodate their pets' needs in style. Pet placemats, bowls, rugs and cushions in playful designs are Ikea's response to consumers' growing desire to spend more on their four-legged friends.

Making the Big Box Beautiful

Ikea cultivates excitement among consumers even at a distance. Witty advertising is amply supported by a mouth-watering catalogue, which presents countless possibilities for home décor renewal. The catalogue is key to Ikea's marketing strategy around the world, helping to build anticipation for the trip to Ikea itself. (It's possible to order items from the catalogue or via the Internet, but Ikea has not traditionally made it easy for customers to arrange for delivery.)

Not only do the big box stores' suburban locations allow the retailer to capitalize on economies of scale, but they actually help cultivate Ikea's status as a true shopping destination. Because only part of the store is warehouse-style, shopping Ikea is more like visiting a theme park of contemporary design than a soul-crushing trip to a utilitarian retail warehouse. The Ikea store layout leads shoppers along a predetermined – one might even say manipulative – path past a range of model interiors that look almost as if people are living in them. Kiosks provide advice on home décor, and colour-coordinated cards suggest ways to combine home décor items.

Each store has a cafeteria serving up bargain-priced Scandinavian specialties

– Swedish meatballs, anyone? – and a children's play area, making Ikea an easy place to while away a couple of hours. Few shopping centres occupy time-pressed shoppers so thoroughly, to say nothing of individual stores.

For all its shopper-friendly qualities, Ikea's emphasis is always on price. Especially low-priced goods, called BTIs ("breathtaking items") in the Ikea culture, are identified by huge yellow price tags. Less breathtaking prices are also prominently displayed, and consistently easy to find. This takes pressure off the relatively scarce sales associates to provide information, and makes it easy for customers to act quickly on their shopping impulses. Ikea pioneered the self-serve environment, yet the majority of its customers are oblivious to this.

Few retailers can boast that shoppers seldom exit their store without making a purchase, but leaving Ikea empty-handed takes more willpower than most consumers possess.

Ikea Psychology

All Ikea's appeal would be for naught if shoppers spent time at the store and not money. But Ikea combines its uniquely alluring shopping experience with a sharp awareness of what consumers want, and what makes them buy.

One thing that makes Ikea a favourite destination is that you know you'll find something you want to buy when you drive there, even if it's merely the Lampan table lamp for $5.99, or the Mixa three-piece set of kitchen utensils for 99 cents.

Low prices like these naturally play an important role in increasing Ikea's popularity. The retailer recognizes that an effective way to increase impulse buying is to offer a broad range of household products for less than $10. The last decade has seen Ikea expand its low-priced offerings in the stationery, tabletop, gift and housewares categories, providing shoppers plenty of opportunities to pick up items that are not only inexpensive, but stylish and practical.

Once a shopper has placed one item in her cart, she is likely to pick up a few more. Perhaps more than any other retailer, Ikea capitalizes on the shopping psychology phenomenon called "the momentum effect." That is, once a shopper has decided to purchase something, her resistance to spending money diminishes, sometimes triggering a shopping spree.

The momentum effect is more than twice as likely to occur when the first item bought is utilitarian, like a cutting board. A self-indulgent purchase – perfume, for instance, which Ikea does not sell – can put a shopper back into a deliberative frame of mind and make her ask herself "Should I buy this?" Because so much of Ikea's offering is practical and priced under $10, consumers routinely enter the store intending to make one small purchase, and end up leaving with a cartload.

As long as Ikea sticks with its current retailing and branding strategies, more consumers will be filling their cart's with its breathtakingly-priced goods. Ikea's quiet takeover of the worldwide furniture and home décor market owes a great deal to the brilliant management of this iconic brand.

THE MODERN BRAND

As Starbucks, Zara and Ikea show, brands that inspire people to buy not only have aspirational qualities, but are supported by products and services that virtually guarantee satisfying transactions.

Using technology to maximize efficiency may be nearly universal in 21st-century retail, but the continuing success of a variety of luxury brands shows that competing on price point is not always the road to success. Brands that support their offering with superior service and store environments earn the right to charge higher prices.

A strong brand can even introduce innovations that change the face of retail forever. Researchers told the late chairman of Sony, Akio Morita, that the original Sony Walkman – one of the most popular gadgets of all time – would never sell. His reply:

"The consumer does not know what is possible. Only we know what is possible."

Do you think Steve Jobs sat around waiting for customers to demand the iPod or the iPhone? Not a chance.

CHAPTER 9

THE LOYALTY MYTH

THE MOBILE CONSUMER

THE 21st century offers a mind-boggling variety of shopping choices. The continuing evolution of the retail landscape encourages exploration, frequently rewarding shoppers with appealing new discoveries.

Well-informed about their options thanks to the Internet, shoppers are driven by an obsession with value and the desire for something new or different, not always because they crave a superior shopping experience. The notion that customers won't defect to a competitor if they're satisfied – also known as loyalty — is largely a myth.

LOYALTY IS SIMPLY THE ABSENCE OF SOMETHING BETTER

These days there is dramatically intensified competition for discretionary spending between stores at traditional regional shopping centres and big box, warehouse or outlet stores, either freestanding or grouped together in power centres. This expansion of new formats has profoundly altered the shopping patterns of many consumers who were once "loyal" to established shopping centres and retailers. The modern consumer splits her time between regular retail stores and a vast range of discount and big box opportunities.

Shopping centres and retailers can do a great deal to minimize customer defection and help ensure shoppers' high expectations are met and even exceeded. In the following pages we explore a number of ways to build the emotional connection with customers that sets one shopping destination apart from another.

By getting to know customers and what they want, retailers and shopping centres can greatly increase people's enjoyment of their shopping experience. Enhancing elements such as signage, décor and service helps keep customers satisfied. When they are truly delighted by what they encounter when they shop your store or centre they're much less likely to defect to your competitors.

Retention vs. Loyalty

Many companies delude themselves by thinking they have a large number of loyal customers, but retention is not the same as loyalty. Customer retention is a question of customer behaviour, while loyalty and relationships are emotional concepts.

Many of the consumers who buy from a company regularly and who appear loyal do not consider themselves loyal at all. Customers who reach the highest levels in customer loyalty programs are often motivated solely by accumulating points. In addition, convenience is often mistaken for loyalty.

Repeat buying behaviour is more accurately described as retention than loyalty. The difficulty for retailers is that customers who buy regularly may go elsewhere as soon as a better bargain or shopping experience comes along.

A truly loyal customer has an emotional bond with a company that will prove enduring. But will a customer pass up a chance to save money because she has an emotional bond with a store? People's shopping habits also change as they move through life's stages, and many consumers abandon old retail favourites as they discover new stores, shopping centres and retail formats that better respond to their current needs.

Any customer's loyalty will be put to the test when a competitor offers a better shopping experience – whether that means better prices, better products or a more engaging shopping environment.

The Challenge of Measuring Loyalty

Is there a measure that can accurately gauge a customer's loyalty? Just as important, do customers really become "emotionally attached" to stores or shopping centres? If so, does that attachment translate into business?

Vague concepts like loyalty will do little for business if customers' basic needs are not being met. The retail cemetery is cluttered with the tombstones of great chains and department stores that claimed to have legions of loyal customers.

Some retailers measure satisfaction with a single survey question. For instance: "Overall, how satisfied would you say you are with your shopping experience at Our Store?" The customer responds by indicating her level of satisfaction on a five- or ten-point scale.

This over-simplified approach provides the company with no direction on how to improve. More precise questions need to be asked when a retailer wants to identify both weak points and strengths.

Focusing on Relationships

The more you know about your customers, the better you can market to them. Customer knowledge is critical to effective marketing and effective customer relationship development.

When attempting to make the most of customer relationships, it is crucial to view the relationship from the customer's perspective. The customer, not the retailer, is the one who decides to form a relationship.

Carefully analyzing the existing customer base can suggest productive directions for targeting new prospects. With vast databases at their disposal, many companies have a tremendous volume of data readily available. Yet businesses need to keep in mind that data and knowledge are two different things.

To become relationship-focused a retailer must move through these stages:

- Customer data
- Information
- Knowledge
- Insight

A relationship is more than the retention of customers or repeat buying. The customer has to feel a relationship. Emphasis on customer service is not the same as emphasis on relationships.

To be relationship-focused, a company must:

- Take a long-term view of customer relationships.

- Believe that building relationships with customers involves more than meeting short-term sales and profit targets.
- Accept that the customer defines the relationship.
- Accept that customer relationships involve an emotional connection.
- Change methods of measuring success, establishing measures that reflect the ability to develop and maintain customer relationships.

Customer Value

Estimates of customer value are usually based on projecting forward recent purchasing patterns, often using the recency-frequency-monetary value model. With sophisticated information systems and cost accounting tools, companies may be able to tell how much profit is made on each sale to a customer, or how potentially "profitable" the customer is.

Examining customers' buying patterns allows you to determine which of the four following categories a customer falls into:

- High volume, high margin
- High volume, low margin
- Low volume, high margin
- Low volume, low margin

Breaking down customer behaviour in this way allows a retailer to aggressively grow existing high-potential customers to greater profitability. Customers can be marketed to differently according to their behaviour.

Some take the position that they should only deal with more profitable customers, but this data-driven definition of customer value is short-sighted. It fails to account for the value of the volume of business a customer may refer or influence because of word-of-mouth. This approach also ignores the future potential of customers, focusing instead on their recent historic value.

Customers who have brought a retailer a substantial volume of business over the years should be rewarded for their loyalty and encouraged to act as ambassadors.

What Is Customer Satisfaction?

Customer satisfaction is a complex concept that is a challenge to quantify. Retailers must be able to identify what exactly customers are satisfied with and what areas need improvement.

There are five main satisfaction drivers in retail:

- **Personal interactions**: Sales associates are friendly, helpful and knowledgeable, anticipating customer needs and exceeding expectations.
- **Environment**: The store or shopping centre is clean, attractive and well laid out, and stores are well stocked, providing enjoyable shopping experiences.
- **Marketing communications**: Promotions are well communicated and valuable to customers.
- **Data analytics**: The store or shopping centre is consistent across all channels in the product information and selection it provides, and offers service that exceeds expectations.
- **Price/value**: The price the customer pays for merchandise is matched or exceeded by the perceived value she receives for the purchase.

Personal interactions and the store environment tend to receive the highest ratings as satisfaction drivers in consumer surveys.

Note that customers with very different priorities – those who insist on good value, for instance, as opposed to those who desire enjoyable interactions with staff – can record the same level of satisfaction in surveys. The nature of a customer's satisfaction must be carefully analyzed if the retailer or shopping centre is to improve its operations in the right way.

Satisfying Customer Relationships

How customers experience a store emotionally directly impacts the level of satisfaction the store can deliver. Consumers have identified four areas as crucial to a sense of shopping satisfaction:

- **Trouble-free shopping**: The retailer meets all expectations and makes the customer feel welcome.

- **Positive associations**: The customer feels the retailer provides the best value compared to competitors, and freely recommends the retailer to family and friends.
- **Feelings of self-esteem**: The customer has the sense she fits in, and feels the store reflects her good judgement.
- **Price enthusiasm**: The customer takes pleasure in taking advantage of the store's low prices and special offers.

Stores and shopping centres need to take steps to enhance their performance on satisfaction drivers and ensure that they consistently deliver all key relationship elements.

MEASURING SATISFACTION

A customer's level of satisfaction is directly proportionate to the gap between what she thinks she will receive from a retailer and what she perceives she is receiving.

To gauge customer satisfaction, retailers need to measure the following areas separately:

- Creating value for customers
- Customer retention
- Creating customer relationships

To improve relationships with customers we need to know not only how we are doing in functional and technical areas but also how customers feel they are being treated, and how they feel about dealing with us. We need to know what we can do to improve their shopping experience, and make them feel better about shopping at our store or shopping centre.

Use the following seven concepts as guidelines when conducting customer satisfaction research:

- Establish clear, achievable goals for every measurement, as well as a baseline for customer satisfaction levels.
- Perform customer satisfaction surveys frequently, because consumer expectations are constantly changing.

- Involve the manager in charge of the area the survey covers, so he or she can take action to improve satisfaction levels.
- Communicate survey results to front-line personnel so they know what they can do to improve customer satisfaction.
- Include customer satisfaction results on the list of key performance indicators reviewed by top executives on a monthly basis.
- Tie staff compensation to customer satisfaction levels and achievement of goals, and evaluate the merit of implementing a bonus program.
- Respond as soon as possible to customer needs identified by the survey, and have survey takers note the source of customers' discontent when they indicate they are "totally dissatisfied."

Providing a satisfying shopping experience creates value for the customer, improves loyalty and strengthens your brand.

Almost Customers

There are consumers who want to shop in our stores, but we make it so difficult or uncomfortable for them that they leave and never return. Plenty of potential customers find their shopping goals frustrated by rude or unknowledgeable staff, inconvenient opening hours, out-of-stocks and other factors that make them walk away without buying.

Could your business be driving away would-be customers?

Thinking Creatively

To gain a competitive advantage retailers need to think creatively, aiming to provide experiences that exceed expectations precisely because they are unexpected.

A true competitive advantage means doing for customers what the competition hasn't thought of doing.

Asking customers how to improve on what you're already doing can only take you so far. Innovative retailers and shopping centres need to try out new ideas and gather data from customers on these initiatives' level of success. A consumer who is pleasantly surprised by the shopping experience you provide is all the more likely to become a loyal customer.

Making Time for Customers

Everyone is pressed for time. As a result the retail industry needs to find creative solutions to meet the needs and maintain the interest of today's diverse and demanding consumers. Anything retailers can do to make life "easier" is welcomed, including one-stop service solutions, longer shopping hours and more experiential retail environments.

A number of innovative retailers and shopping centres have taken steps to make shopping quicker, easier and more enjoyable for their customers. A range of initiatives such as shopping centre concierges, improved signage and enjoyable events help save customers time and enhance the shopping experience.

The Shopping Centre Concierge

In the U.S., the length of a shopper's average mall visit has been flat or declining for years. More than two in five shoppers are estimated to leave the typical shopping centre without making a non-food purchase.

Every extra minute a shopper spends in the mall means extra sales. Therefore it's up to shopping centres to find innovative ways of encouraging shoppers to **linger longer**.

The solution? Provide accommodating services that enhance the customer experience at the shopping centre level, according to property management companies including Westfield America and Macerich. By hiring concierges to assist shoppers at many of their properties, these companies aimed to increase the convenience and pleasure customers experience at their centres, in the hope they'll stay longer and spend more.

What does a concierge do?

- Offer to carry bags
- Push strollers
- Make restaurant, spa and show ticket reservations
- Sell postage stamps
- Send faxes

- Book rental cars
- Carry hand-held computers that can print coupons for centre tenants
- Hand out bottled water, key chains, diapers and baby wipes, gummy bears, balloons, lip-gloss, M&Ms or Advil.
- Speak more than one language: Cantonese or French, for example.

Westfield's concierges are assigned to make contact with 100 to 150 shoppers and five retailers on every eight-hour shift.

The company claims their concierge initiative, known internally as Westfield Wow, makes shoppers stay longer and buy more. Westfield claims the average customer expenditure went from just under US$100 to slightly less than $125 following the program's implementation. Shoppers spent less than 90 minutes per visit before the concierges arrived on the scene, while after they appeared average visitation increased by almost an hour.

Westfield found the marketing funds to pay for the concierge program by dropping special events such as fashion shows, which drove traffic but also irritated regular customers, who couldn't find parking. **The company allocated over half of its advertising budget to the new initiative, since Westfield executives had concluded that buying radio and television advertising had a negligible effect on increasing spending at Westfield centres.**

Delighting Holiday Shoppers

Note that Westfield initiated its concierge program during the holiday season, the time of year when harried shoppers most appreciate extra care and attention. Like attentive service, holiday décor plays a critical role in encouraging customers to take genuine pleasure in their shopping excursions, and helps to build emotional connections with a shopping centre.

Few argue with the notion that well-conceived holiday décor package and a well-planned agenda of holiday events help create the right atmosphere for holiday shopping, and can even build an air of anticipation that makes consumers excited about shopping a destination.

In decades past, department stores in cities across North America prided themselves on their lavish holiday window displays. Appreciative crowds came to marvel at the twinkling, carefully crafted Christmas scenes. This century, most shopping centres put up decorations with the aim of creating a festive atmosphere, but few reshape themselves into unique holiday destinations that truly delight shoppers.

Ambitious décor programs successfully transform holiday shopping into an eagerly anticipated experience. This approach stands in contrast to the considerably more utilitarian holiday shopping environments offered by price-obsessed big-box destinations.

TIME-SAVING SIGNAGE

We've all had the experience of being unable to find what we want in a store due to inadequate or confusing signage. Signage is a basic customer comfort issue that has a direct relationship to profitability, yet many retailers ignore the importance of quality signs.

Researchers at Wal-Mart discovered in interviews with customers that there was the potential to improve store signage through better placement and less clutter. Shoppers asked for signs down the aisles: goosenecks positioned about every eight feet that show what's on offer. Time-pressed consumers like to be able to find what they're looking for quickly, rather than searching up and down each aisle.

When these changes were implemented as a test program, shoppers immediately found the improved signage practical and relevant. Navigating was easier, shopping was more efficient and shoppers relied less on staff. Overall, the changes made a favourable impact on customer perceptions of the store's quality, and Wal-Mart enhanced its competitive advantage by making shopping easier, and saving customers time.

SATISFIED CUSTOMERS AT WILLIAMS-SONOMA

Williams-Sonoma customers are exceptionally satisfied with their shopping experiences. According to surveys, more than three-quarters give the stores high marks for neatness, while nearly half rate the retailer highly for providing an entertaining shopping experience.

Stores provide relevant, interesting in-store events to develop customers. For example, the retailer identified a group of customers who had purchased gifts through the online bridal registry and invited them to attend cooking lessons and demonstrations. This promotion enhanced the store's brand while attracting cooking enthusiasts, a profitable customer segment.

Retailers can do the following to emulate the Williams-Sonoma example:

- Enhance stores' attractiveness – customers notice the difference. This is a key differentiating point between top performers and lesser competitors.
- Market and merchandise stores according to customer insights, instead of relying on a standard assortment triangle of high to low price-point items.
- Pay careful attention to the most enthusiastic and profitable customers, and deliver the experience that delights them.

Customer Defection: Winning Them Back

In the increasingly competitive retail marketplace there's always the very real possibility of losing loyal customers. The average business loses 20 to 40 per cent of its customers every year. This is a serious loss, because the mature customer's profit contribution is much higher than that of a customer who has only been buying for a year or two.

When a long-term customer defects, the profitability deficit left behind can't be made up by simply recruiting a new customer. This makes win-back programs a valuable investment.

The best customers are well worth winning back – partly because their numbers are relatively small. In most categories, a third of the buyers account for two-thirds of the purchases. In addition, the high profit segment delivers six to ten times as much profit as the low profit segment. It's crucial to win back these long-term, high-profit customers when you lose them.

Never Ignore a Lost Customer

In addition to lost revenue, customer defection can result in the following:

- Each lost customer is potentially an ambassador of bad news. The

Internet gives them the opportunity to complain vocally in a very public forum.
- When you try to win back these customers, you often cancel out any past negativity by showing the customer she is missed, even if your win-back attempt proves unsuccessful.
- Surveys show the primary reason for customer defection is "no special reason." This means the retailer took the customer for granted and made it easy for her to leave.

Customer retention efforts need to be backed up with win-back programs that quickly recapture your best customers.

The Rewards of Win-Back

Lost customers are far from a lost cause. Customers who have already shopped your store or shopping centre know your brand, so when you communicate with them they're more likely to listen than new prospects, who lack familiarity with what you offer.

In fact, companies have a much better chance of winning business from lost customers than from prospects, and reactivation promotions typically outperform prospect promotions.

The average retailer has:

- A 60 to 70 per cent probability of making a successful sale to an active customer.
- A 20 to 40 per cent probability with a lost customer.
- A less than 20 per cent probability of successfully selling to a prospect.

In some cases it's possible to prevent customer defection altogether. That's why it's crucial to address challenges with active customers as soon as you can. Track their purchasing behaviours, taking note of lagging visits and low purchase rates. When you lose a customer, conduct an exit interview if possible to find out why.

A sample exit interview might go like this:

"Hello Mrs. Goodshopper, I'm calling from Our Retailer. Our records show we haven't served you in more than a year. Whenever a valued customer like you stops shopping with us we get concerned…"

How to Win Them Back

Customers can be segmented according to their reason for defecting. There are five defector categories:

1. **Intentionally pushed-away customers**, who are unprofitable to serve. This will become a growth area as technology easily identifies chronic return abuse.
2. **Unintentionally pushed-away customers**, who left because their expectations weren't met.
3. **Pulled-away customers**, who have been lured away by competitors offering better value, often beyond better price.
4. **Bought-away customers**, who are price-driven and can be won over with low-ball introductory offers.
5. **Moved-away customers**, whose needs have changed due to age, lifestyle or geographical changes.

Unintentionally pushed-away and pulled-away customers make the best win-back prospects.

Lost Customers: Steps to Recovery

A customer's second life cycle can differ markedly from the first life cycle because the customer knows more about the retailer's products than a new prospect, and the retailer has more data about the customer's preferences. In addition, the personal recognition shown by a successful win-back could spur the customer to greater spending.

It's extremely important to find out as much as possible about your lost customers and why they stopped buying from you. Focus groups among lost customers are one way of finding out why they went to the competition. Once you know why competitors' offerings were perceived as more attractive, make the necessary changes and let these customers know you're working on correcting the problems they've pinpointed. This is the key to rebuilding trust, and trust is crucial to the emotional connection otherwise known as loyalty.

Ten Relationship Marketing Truths

Customers are not loyal. They actively seek out better bargains and new ways to shop. Traditional loyalty factors such as friendly, customized sales service no longer count for as much as they once did. Today's customer is never satisfied, and is in control of the selling process. Competitors are just a mouse-click away.

Companies want relationships, but customers don't. Bombarded with telemarketing calls, junk mail and spam, many consumers don't want relationships with retailers or shopping centres. A relationship marketing program can only extend the life of a customer if management understands what drives the relationship, such as products or customer service.

Customers love information. A retailer or shopping centre that keeps its name in front of the customer can extend that customer's life cycle. Retail businesses need to expand and maximize their communications networks to cover the wide variety of touchpoints customers may use.

Customers are in charge of the selling process. Internet research allows consumers to evaluate a number of options before making a purchase. Pricing and loyalty programs need to provide real value as compared to competitors' offerings.

Think of your lifetime value to the customer, not the customer's lifetime value to your store. Companies need to know their customers' demographics and purchases and use this information to improve the chance of marketing to them effectively. Customers must also be given options for customizing the email communications you send them. Through rewards and targeted communications a company can extend its lifetime value in the customer's eyes.

Keep your loyalty rewards program simple. Customers don't spend more because there are different reward levels for different levels of spending. Complicated loyalty rewards programs also confuse and frustrate sales associates.

Reporting must focus on the customer. Management should keep sight of the reporting focus and establish clear and measurable reporting benchmarks for their program. Accurate reporting is the key to understanding customer behaviour and shifting buying patterns.

Think creatively. Test a variety of offers for different groups of customers and see how they react. If a certain offer triggers a positive response, expand the program.

Customers expect to be thanked. The customer's wish to be thanked should be regarded as an expectation. Your expression of gratitude can take the form of a simple follow-up thank-you letter after the first major purchase. Loyalty programs thank customers for continued patronage: "**spend and earn, redeem and save**." Both monetary and soft rewards have their place in marketing plans.

All customers have potential. Retailers who focus exclusively on their "most valuable" customers and ignore others should consider the following:

» Your "less valuable" customers can buy more
» Your "most valuable" customers can leave
» Browsers can become customers
» Lost customers can be won back
» Unhappy customers can post complaints online

Managing customer relationships requires technical discipline, customer-centred thinking and a willingness to try out new ideas. The goal is to deliver sustainable, profitable growth by marketing to known customers in a way that your competition will scramble to mimic.

The mantra of today's consumer:

"**My expectations are hardly unreasonable.**"

DOES LOYALTY EXIST?

At the end of the twentieth century, technology accelerated the rate of change in retail, especially in terms of new shopping formats and the availability of information on the Internet. Consumers these days are not inherently less loyal than in the past; instead, they're keeping up with changes in the retail landscape by exploring the variety of options on offer.

As a retailer or shopping centre, I urge you to focus on developing and promoting the facets of your unique offering and shopping environment that contribute to customer satisfaction. When shoppers are delighted each time they visit your store or shopping centre – and when you repeatedly exceed their expectations – they may become loyal customers after all.

CHAPTER 10

EMPOWERED CONSUMERS

WHAT WE WANT

THE 21st century is the century of too much of everything. Industries struggle with overcapacity, and everywhere there is a surplus of information.

Advertisers also have difficulty reaching ad-saturated consumers. With the proliferation of new communications channels, from Internet-enabled cell phones to digital cable channels, it's increasingly difficult for marketers to communicate effectively with the masses.

The way we have responded as consumers to the over-abundance of both information and merchandise is to embrace the notion of ourselves as "special." People today want retailers to respect their individuality. To even catch our attention, advertisers need to make the effort to talk to each of us one-to-one. As a result, individual consumers wield more power than ever before.

TOMORROW'S CUSTOMER

Customers are more demanding than ever, more contradictory, and more difficult to identify. Tomorrow's retail leaders will be those that are truly customer-centred, enabling them to meet customers' expectations in terms of product, service and store environment.

Our studies of the marketplace have revealed the following consumer mega-trends:

1. **Multicultural Mosaic**

   The North America composed of nuclear families of mostly European ancestry has ceased to exist, especially in large urban centres. More than ever, our society is made up of diverse and multi-ethnic households.

The term "family" is also being redefined. It can mean single-parent families, same-sex couples and extended families that include grandparents and even friends. As a society we have become more aware of, and sensitive to, diversity and individual differences. Retailers must respect this.

2. **Customers Without Cues**

   Age, sex and style of dress no longer provide clear cues to a customer's lifestyle or spending power. Children are assuming more adult roles, while adults mimic youth trends. There are stay-at-home dads and CEO moms. Knock-off items make it hard to judge a customer's level of affluence by her appearance.

   The new customer has a shorter attention span, less patience and less civility than the traditional customer. She has better access to information, and will take the initiative to get what she wants.

   Beware of assuming anything about your customers – you might end up losing their business.

3. **Consumer Power**

   Consumers now have more power than ever, and they put that power to use to make better purchase decisions and receive better service. Because of the Internet, many consumers know almost everything about products and services before even entering a store, enabling them to easily assess the fairness of a transaction. They will make these assessments even more readily in the future.

   Today's consumers are very conscious of the value of time, and impatient with anyone who wastes it. They are also aware of the value of their patronage to retailers, and expect something in return. They seek more control, demanding more forms of customization and desiring to dictate the pace of their shopping experience.

4. **Leaving choice to the experts**

   The sheer number of brands in the marketplace contributes to a glut in consumers' minds. With too many options, making choices becomes increasingly difficult. This is why people look to experts like Oprah Winfrey to find out what issues they should be interested in, and what they should read. In an over-complicated world, consumers yearn for fewer, not more choices, so they seek out advocates who can steer them through the chaos.

5. **The multiple-community, multiple-personality shopper**
   In our information and product-saturated world, consumers are using technology to divide themselves into a number of different virtual personas, and are enthusiastic about products that allow them to change identities, such as role-playing computer games. Marketers must keep in mind that each customer is really several different customers, fitting into a number of segmentation models.
   Clubs, online communities, neighbourhood associations, volunteer groups and other forms of community are proliferating. Internet access, the rise in single-person households and an increased sense of alienation are driving people to become members of new communities. Consumers – especially youth – tend to belong to several different communities at once.

Mass Marketing in Decline

The complex nature of the modern consumer reflects the decline of the mass market. Countless niche markets have emerged, making narrower and more accurate targeting a must for marketers. Retailers, meanwhile, must ensure their offering is carefully edited and suited to the current tastes of their customer base.

In the golden age of the mass market, the Big Three TV networks in the U.S. – CBS, NBC and ABC – united the consumer market to a degree likely never to be rivalled again. In that era, an advertiser could reach four in five American women with an ad aired on the three networks simultaneously. Today, an advertiser would need to run the ad on at least a hundred TV channels to reach such a wide audience. No alternative medium can hope to match the ubiquity of network television in its prime.

Today's consumer market consists of a bewildering and constantly

evolving mosaic of audience micro-segments that marketers have an increasingly difficult job keeping track of, much less reaching.

Marketers have had to shift their focus from selling to millions of anonymous consumers to selling to millions of individual consumers. "Relevance" is key: if you can't make your product or service offering relevant to your customer's lifestyle, you have little hope of attracting that customer's business. The quest for relevance has led big companies to shift the focus of their media buy away from old mass market media such as TV, and invest more in advertising that targets niche markets.

The North American market has atomized into micro-segments characterized by well-defined yet subtly nuanced preferences. Marketers now need to make intelligent use of the increasing range of communications options new technology provides. Simultaneously, consumers' use of new technologies makes consumer preferences harder to keep track of.

In addition, many people no longer wish to see themselves as belonging to a mass market. Personalization and opportunities for self-expression are increasingly valued, especially among younger consumers. Many desire products and services that are adapted to their own needs and preferences. New technology has made increased customization an important trend, especially where media consumption is concerned.

In his influential 1993 book *Mass Customization*, author Joe Pine wrote that "Companies have to get out of the commoditization trap, and one way of doing that is customizing that product down to the individual."

To understand how a particular consumer segment values customization, however, we need to take a close look at this popular catch phrase. Some of what is being labelled "customization" is merely choice – and abundant choice is something affluent W

THE MYTH OF MASS CUSTOMIZATION

The idea of mass customization has been so popular over the last decade that product selection is sometimes incorrectly called customization. I recently read an article that held up the fact that iPods were available in a range of colours as "customization." We would have to go back to the days of the Model T Ford (available only in black for most of its production run) to find mass-produced items manufactured without regard for consumer preferences in colour and style.

A famous example of an attempt to make customization available via the Internet is fashion merchant Land's End. The retailer went to great lengths to overcome consumers' reluctance to buy clothes online by incorporating customizing technology into its website. Building on the foundation of its well-developed catalogue business, Land's End implemented its revolutionary My Virtual Model technology in 1998.

My Virtual Model allows patrons to build an online version of themselves – with similar measurements, at least – that can try on the company's styles. This innovation aimed to take the guesswork out of ordering clothes online, allowing customers to feel more confident in their purchases.

However, the flurry of positive press around My Virtual Model subsided after 2001 or so. Later in the decade, the men's Custom Clothing page on landsend.com was advising customers to "complete a brief online profile by answering a few simple fit questions." The page also included a reassurance that "you won't need to take any complicated measurements." It's possible that male shoppers, at least, generally lacked the detailed knowledge of their measurements to create a virtual model.

A new focus on the website on Live Help (by phone or online chat) suggests many customers prefer to pick up the phone and talk to a customer service representative, rather than invest valuable time in a more involved approach to customization. Indeed, e-commerce success story Zappos.com has built its success partly on ensuring phone support is available to customers 24/7.

When Land's End was bought by Sears in 2002, My Virtual Model became a feature of the parent company's fashion e-tailing as well. Sears hoped incorporating Land's End's e-tailing expertise would make the company's e-commerce operations more competitive, especially in the fashion category.

It's worth noting that leading fashion sites such as BananaRepublic.com take a more straightforward approach to customization. The online shopper chooses from a limited range of styles, colours and sizes, much as customers have always done when selecting fashions.

Inventions and innovations that catch on typically save people money, add convenience, or both. If a consumer finds using technology more time-consuming or complicated than selecting a size and colour in a more traditional way, its novelty will quickly wear off.

Price vs. Customization

Traditionally, customization has cost extra. Current technology allows companies like Nike to allow consumers to create personalized running shoe designs, which would hardly have been possible a generation ago. But while anyone with Internet access may enjoy picking out a unique running shoe colour palette, far fewer consumers will be willing to pay over US$100 to have the shoes made.

Customized fashions appeal both to self-styled trendsetters and to marketers, who value the media coverage and cachet these initiatives can generate. "Customization" has become such a popular buzzword in the past decade that marketers may well over-estimate consumer demand for it. Particularly in times of economic instability, the sale-price obsession of the average consumer means she will not happily pay a premium, or even full-price, for most items.

In an era of disposable fashions, many would rather buy the latest thing at H&M than wait even a few weeks for a custom-made item to be delivered. Thanks to their sophisticated supply chain technologies, fast fashion retailers effectively customize clothes to the tastes of relatively narrow market niches, getting designs into their stores almost before consumers know they want them.

As for home décor, a degree of customization has always been demanded by affluent consumers. Custom fabric options have long been the norm for upholstered furniture, and the custom kitchen has recently enjoyed a renaissance.

Then there is monogrammed merchandise. Williams-Sonoma, for instance, offers monogrammed flatware, linens and doormats. Retailers will increasingly embrace this kind of customization where it can provide a competitive advantage in a cost-effective way.

Where customization will have a large impact on most consumers is in the consumption of media. People increasingly expect to be able to enjoy the content of their choice on the device of their choice.

Many consumers would rather compile their own MP3 play list than fast-forward through music tracks on a CD. Many would rather watch a TV episode on YouTube than sit through endless TV commercials. This kind of customization costs the user very little or nothing, and adds to the convenience people enjoy in consuming media. The popularity of user-designed media experiences – more than user-designed merchandise – will continue to grow rapidly.

Too Much Choice

Because consumers would now rather be "special" than "normal," companies have created a bewildering array of products and services targeted at every conceivable micro-niche. TNS Media Intelligence adds 700 brands per day to the 2 million already in its database.

Product proliferation has created the challenge of finding buyers in a market defined by excess choice. Ironically, today's market is also full of virtually identical products, from the dollar store to the luxury level.

Ultimately, the overabundance of choice is one of the great challenges of modern consumption, and many shoppers experience considerable agony over having to make choices. In this age of micro-markets, what people often yearn for is less choice, not more.

On my visits to stores and shopping centres around the world, I have repeatedly seen consumers crippled by indecision. Regardless of their level of intelligence, consumers do not always choose well. Unable or unwilling to choose for themselves, they often prefer to let inertia take over. Every day, millions of customers around the world leave stores empty-handed for fear of making the wrong choice.

Micromarketing

The decline of mass marketing has been underway for decades. Both newspaper circulation and prime-time network TV ratings have been decreasing since the 1970s. Speeding this decline is the proliferation of wireless communications and digital networks, fragmenting yesterday's mass audience into micro-audiences tuned to narrowcast satellite TV and radio channels, not to mention computer, PDA and cell-phone screens.

Factor in thousands of specialized magazines that have largely replaced the old general-interest titles, and you have a media landscape in which the average person's attention is fragmented into increasingly minuscule units.

The most effective way to respond to the fragmentation of audiences and markets? Micromarketing.

It is no longer economically feasible to send a message to the masses in the hope of reaching individuals. Consequently, finding the best way and best time to communicate with consumers is crucial. Without the existence of a mass market, marketing messages that miss their mark are apt to miss it entirely.

How Technology Changed a Generation

Younger people are generally the first to adopt new technologies. Text messaging, for instance, quickly caught on with teens and developed its own unique slang, while many older folk viewed the skill of "texting" as too time-consuming to pick up.

Millennials – the generation coming of age in the new millennium, born between 1979 and 1994 – have grown up with the Internet and are adept at using a range of digital media. As a result they tend to see information as something they can control.

This is also the generation marketers fret about reaching, because they're quick to employ a variety of technological means to avoid advertising they're not interested in. They deftly skip boring TV commercials by channel surfing and zapping with a TiVo remote. They're quick to kill online pop-ups with a blocker unless the pop-up makes them an appealing offer.

Millennials are renowned for multitasking, and are likely to devour several types of communication and media simultaneously – for example, by chatting online while watching one or more TV shows. The old barriers between media hardly exist for this generation: the computer functions as both a stereo and TV, game consoles are connected to the Internet, and cell phones are used to take pictures and post them to social networking sites.

While the Internet has become almost ubiquitous across age and income groups, teens and young adults are still the quickest to embrace new technologies. In developed economies, college-age students are at the forefront of the digital communication revolution.

This is great news for gadget retailers, but youth's appetite for this digital smorgasbord creates challenges for marketers. With more than half of 13- to 24-year-olds watching TV and surfing the net at the same time, not to mention the distractions of cell phones and video games, advertisers are starting to blend promotions through a variety of media.

Viewers wishing to cast a vote in the Fox network's *American Idol*, for instance, do so using AT&T Wireless cell phone text messages. Because young people's attention is seldom focused on the TV, advertisers are turning increasingly to product placement and other approaches to embedding ads, such as digital billboards at sports events.

Marketers also leverage the common desire among young people to be among the first to know about something – for example, to see a popular DVD before their friends do. When marketers succeed at making a product part of a younger consumer's world, word-of-mouth takes care of the rest, because they're eager to talk about their discoveries with friends.

Efforts to market to this group are also prone to pitfalls. Websites that ask for personal information often leave younger visitors cold, because people in this group are well aware their personal data may be used for marketing things to them. Advertisers that fail to make a good first impression will in future be blocked or zapped.

This generation is prepared to spend money on products marketed to their desires and preferences, but they demand options, and will soak up only information that strikes them as useful. Advertisers who cater to this group's enthusiasm for customizing and controlling information, and who embrace the fragmented nature of the digital marketplace, have the potential to succeed in an ad-saturated world.

The New Family

One of the challenges for researchers is figuring out the direction consumer trends will take, given the changing makeup of the family unit. The Canadian birthrate is at its lowest level ever, households are smaller and families spend less time together. Women with more than two children living at home are relatively rare, census figures from Statistics Canada show. Today's family is markedly different from the family of even a decade ago.

The fact that families are smaller is only one of the factors contributing to the shrinking size of households, however. Childless couples, single parents and lone homeowners are on the rise. Singles of all ages are becoming an increasingly important consumer group, with their own set of household needs and desires.

Adult children are also staying at home longer, or returning home after a few years on their own. Two in five young adults aged 20 to 29 are still living with their parents, compared to just over a quarter in 1981.

While the average person born in the 1950s left home at the age of 21, today's 20-somethings are less likely to move far away from their parents, largely due to a lack of cash. High student debt loads – often in the neighbourhood of $40,000 for a university graduate – contribute to this delayed transition into full adulthood. Some young adults move back in with their parents when a relationship fails, or when a job loss makes solo living unaffordable. Staying on a few more years with Mom and Dad often makes financial sense.

Putting off full adulthood also means putting off marriage and child-bearing, which has a negative effect on fertility rates. About half of women over forty are infecund, meaning that couples that delay having children may risk being unable to conceive at all.

Meanwhile, technology is contributing to a disconnect between family members. While Mom watches TV and Dad interfaces with his Blackberry, the kids are chatting online.

To create quality time, families are making "dates" outside the home. This could mean a day trip, a family ski package or simply dinner out. Even luxury services like spa treatments, traditionally intended for adult women, are increasingly popular among parents who want to share time relaxing with their children.

18 to 34: Myth and Reality

Younger consumers continue to be the most coveted by advertisers – even if there's not much reason for that anymore.

For decades, marketers have been obsessed with the under-35 set. "If we can get them young we've got them for life" is one school of thought. "Older consumers are attracted to products that have a youthful image" is another. This kind of thinking has held sway ever since the vast buying power of the boomer generation first attracted advertisers' attention in the '60s.

In reality, people over 50 now account for half of all the discretionary spending in the U.S. Proportionally, there are more of them than ever, and they watch more TV, go to more movies and buy more CDs than young people. Yet North Americans over 50 are the target of less than 10 per cent of the advertising.

The tendency of marketers and advertisers to ignore older consumers has its roots in the demographics of the U.S. in the '60s and '70s. By 1966, 48 per cent of Americans were under the age of 25, and advertisers scrambled to talk their language at the risk of alienating this vast segment. Advertisers prized youth's obsession with "revolution" and suggested a friendship between advertisers and the young, a friendship that was fictional but seemed cool. The way to get in on this friendship was, of course, to buy the product being advertised.

Advertisers remained obsessed with the 18-to-34 demographic for the next three decades.

Television suddenly became research-driven and demographically self-conscious by the early '70s, and most entertainment is research-driven now. *Star Wars,* released in 1977, marked the beginning of films acting as ads for their own merchandise.

Meanwhile, the boomers' demographic bubble floated upwards, and no one seemed to notice. More Americans were over 65, and median real income for families with children headed by people under 30 fell dramatically. Households headed by a 55-to-64-year-old have a median net worth at least fifteen times the net worth of the average under-35 household.

Additionally, pop culture is no longer just for the young. Over the last decade, the proportion of the national movie audience between the ages of 50 and 59 doubled, while the proportion of teenagers shrank steadily. The per centage of CDs sold to consumers over 45 also doubled.

Nonetheless, advertisers continue to romanticize youth, using the terms "hard-to-reach" and "coveted" to describe the 18-to-34s. Yet there are proportionally fewer young people than there used to be, and they have less money than they used to.

Why do advertisers continue to court the youth demographic so obsessively? Don't they know that 50 is the new 38?

Courting the Mature Woman

Many a boomer woman experienced a sense of frustration when she grew into middle age and discovered, after being wooed by marketers all her adult life, that she was no longer the ad industry's darling. New gadgets were consistently marketed to younger people. Worse, it was impossible to find contemporary fashions that fit her figure and didn't make her look like a wannabe teenager. Today's 50-year-old woman doesn't want to be dowdy, a fact many retailers have overlooked.

Only now is retail starting to wake up to the realities of a more mature consumer.

One American chain that has been courting the mature woman for over two decades is Chico's, with more than 1,000 women's specialty stores selling private label apparel in 49 states. Chico's achieves double-digit revenue growth in stores open at least a year based on the straightforward formula of providing current fashions that fit. According to customers, Chico's clothes allow a 50-year-old woman to look up-to-the-minute without feeling ridiculous.

Big names like Ralph Lauren, Calvin Klein, Ann Taylor and the Jones Apparel Group also ship lines aimed at the mature woman. A considerable range of styles is on offer, each line embodying its own vision of what the mature woman wants. The customer of traditionalist retailer Talbot's might feel most at home at the garden club, while Ann Taylor's clothes are more fitted and career-oriented. Calvin Klein caters to the urban sophisticate, and Ralph Lauren to the socialite.

For marketers, the challenge is to reach the mature customer without making younger consumers think the brand is uncool. Research has revealed, however, that ads featuring older people can appeal even to youthful consumers.

In addition, the notion of older people taking part in sports and strenuous outdoors activities is no longer surprising to North American ad audiences. The active lifestyles of the older set have even prompted marketing execs to rename this generation "zoomers."

It's clear that thinking about the needs and wants of well-heeled zoomers will soon become the norm for ad executives and marketers, much as ignoring them used to be second nature.

RETIREMENT IS GOLDEN

While adult children are staying at home longer, their parents are staying in the workforce well past the traditional age of retirement. In fact, late-nesting adult children can create a financial burden that may delay their parents' retirement savings goals. Seniors these days can't always expect to have financed their retirement by their early 60s, especially given the probable length of it.

What's more, the old enthusiasm for abandoning work late in life has faded, as more boomers opt to keep working as long as they can. This is in part because the older set no longer views retirement as a time to downsize and live frugally.

There has been a marked shift in the way older people think about their retirement lifestyle, and many who have achieved a level of affluence during their working lives have no intention of giving that up once they leave the workforce. Scrimping and saving may be second nature to many born before the Second World War, but boomers have indulged themselves throughout their lives, and are not prepared to cut down on indulgences in retirement.

The seniors of the future may abandon highly stressful full-time careers at retirement age, but many will help support their lifestyles by working in less demanding jobs – as researchers or teaching assistants, for example.

Meanwhile, ageing boomers spend increasing amounts on the upmarket goods and services younger people can't yet afford. Renovating is big with this set: some feather their recently emptied nests with top-of-the-line appliances and expensive fixtures. A small group have become serial renovators. Others buy the sports cars they've always dreamed of owning.

One thing many empty nesters worry little about is providing their children with a substantial inheritance. According to one model, perfect financial planning means running out of money right when you die. Living lavishly in the senior years does tend to mean leaving less to pass down.

Grandparents Raising Grandchildren

Many seniors benefit from co-habiting with family: nearly half a million Canadian grandparents live in households with their children and grandchildren. The extended family has new relevance now that many working parents rely on in-laws to help look after their kids. According to Canada's 2006 census, over half of grandparents live in multi-generational homes with their adult children, their spouses and their grandchildren.

Grandparents these days are healthier than in previous generations, and better able to play an active role in the household. Grandparents in immigrant families are twice as likely as the Canadian-born to live in multi-generational households and take care of grandchildren. Those who worked long hours earlier in life and couldn't spend much time with their children are eager to play a role in the lives of their grandchildren. In some cases, grandparents help keep families together by caring for grandchildren after a divorce.

Grandparents are sometimes financially responsible for the household, especially when living with a single parent, or when raising grandchildren without the parents' involvement. Roles in multi-generational families are apt to become blurred over time, with grandparents acting as both caregivers and care recipients.

All of this suggests the retail industry should view grandparents in a new light. The nuclear family has to some extent been replaced by the multi-generational household, in which grandparents play a central role.

SHOPPING FOR ONE

One of the most significant trends emerging from recent census data is the shift toward single-person households. There are now as many single-person households in Canada as there are households of four or more people. Twenty years ago, one-person households accounted for one-fifth of all households, whereas now they account for one-quarter.

Retail sectors that cater to the needs of the single person welcome this trend. Since singles often have pets, it's great news for pet food manufacturers. Appliance manufacturers also benefit from higher demand for individual units.

Younger singles (under 35) spend more on personal enjoyment. For 35-to-54-year-old singles, items like laundry care products are sought after, since people in this group tend to be homebodies.

Older singles, aged 55 and up, tend to spend more heavily on value-added beauty and health products. (Singles in all age groups spend more on appearance and health matters than non-singles.) Other items favoured by older singles include luxury goods such as gourmet cooking oils and coffee products. In part due to the climbing retirement age, many in this group also have a home office, so some of their discretionary dollars go to office-related items.

MARKETING TO CULTURAL DIVERSITY

Many of today's North American consumers were born in other countries, and marketers are divided on how to reach them. While some believe in marketing to non-native English speakers in their own language, many recent immigrants are eager to adopt the styles and attitudes of their new country, and are often most easily reached by mainstream marketing efforts.

Diversity may at first glance seem to justify "ethnic" marketing, or marketing based on the consumer's ancestry. But consumers' shopping patterns are rarely a product of ancestry alone. In the global village, people are not defined by their ancestry any more than by their age or their generation. Consumer behaviour is in fact determined by the individual's unique combination of age, ancestry, heritage, education, income, life experience, and fundamental values.

Culture defines consumer behaviour, and culture includes values, interests, lifestyles, beliefs and aspirations.

People in North America today are multi-cultural, not mono-cultural.

Contemporary marketing is inherently multicultural, because we live in a multicultural world. Multicultural marketing concentrates on learning about consumers rather than imposing definitions on them.

Consumers belong to many different groups of shared interests simultaneously, and can be influenced at any given moment by a whole range of contexts: ancestral contexts, peer contexts and career contexts, as well as spur-of-the-moment impulses.

Effective market analysis combines information about age, generational cohort and ancestry with cultural attributes such as values, tastes, beliefs, interests and attitudes. From the increasing diversity and fragmentation of consumer markets, market researchers need to work hard to find the common threads that connect the diverse strands of a given market.

Advertising in a Fragmented Age

Media fragmentation has created micro-audiences that can be reached only by narrowly targeted campaigns. How are advertisers and marketers going to deal with this challenging scenario in the coming decade?

Airing a spot on network TV during prime time has become prohibitively expensive, despite the fact that audiences have been declining since the 1970s. While prime-time ratings fell about 42 per cent between 1977 and 2003, network TV's ad revenues went up nearly five times.

The 80th Anniversary edition of the Academy Awards in 2008 garnered the smallest U.S. audience of any Oscars broadcast since viewer totals were fist recorded in 1974. Nonetheless, the show remains the year's highest-rated entertainment special, and is a cash cow for Walt Disney Co.'s ABC. The company raked in an average of US$1.8-million for each 30-second commercial, up 7 per cent from 2007.

Marketers who make television part of their media buy are effectively paying more for less. The range of prime-time advertising, in the U.S. at least, has narrowed considerably, so networks' revenues are now heavily dependent on just four industries: telecommunications, pharmaceuticals, cars and movies.

Putting aside the astronomical expense of buying airtime on major networks, the popularity of YouTube and the proliferation of ad-zapping Personal Video Recorders (PVRs) like TiVo enables more consumers to steer clear of TV ads. Channel surfing during ad breaks grew out of the widespread use of the remote control; further technological advances allow savvy TV watchers to enjoy their programs free of breaks altogether.

Rather than relying on old-fashioned mass media, marketers have boosted spending on more targetable narrowcast media, and will continue to do so. Some predict that by 2010 marketers will be spending more on Internet advertising than on either network TV or magazines.

The fact is, TV technology does not permit the interactivity that enables narrow targeting. Direct mail, email, telemarketing, in-store displays and closed-circuit TV are some of the methods marketers are turning to in order to reach closely targeted groups effectively. One-to-many communications are being replaced by a variety of forms of one-to-one communications. In the future, ads that grab your attention will often not look like any ad you've seen before – and may not even look like ads at all.

MAGAZINES FOR SHOPPERS

Print, arguably the oldest of the mass media, has evolved rapidly to meet the needs of the fragmented consumer landscape. Hundreds of new magazines are created each year.

A generation or two ago, general-interest titles like *Time*, *Look* and *Life* dominated the print market. These days, only about one in ten of the thousands of titles published in North America can be considered general interest, down from almost a third a mere two decades ago.

Among the most successful of the new crop of specialty publications are the shopping magazines, which aim to turn fashion fantasies into purchases. Condé Nast's *Lucky* is the most celebrated of a host of international shopping titles, with a circulation of 1.1 million by 2008.

In a shopping magazine editorial is largely eliminated, as are traditional high fashion spreads. The focus is merchandise: multi-page spreads of cosmetics, jewelry, bags, coats and, of course, shoes. Shopping for these items is made easy because details like price and store locations are provided. *Lucky* invites readers to mark the things they like by providing stickers marked "Maybe?" and "Yes!"

While the traditional fashion magazine is mostly aspirational, the shopping magazine aims to answer the question "Where can I buy this?" The clothes in fashion magazines might not be available at a nearby shopping centre, but shopping magazines tell the reader exactly where to find items. This is why the publishers claim the magazines do a great job of motivating consumption.

Condé Nast also publishes *Domino*, a home décor shopping magazine targeting women consumers with above-average household incomes. *Cargo*, a shopping magazine for male readers, folded in 2006 after a two-year run.

Lucky's readership also has the option of visiting the magazine's website, luckymag.com. With circulation of the magazine largely stable during the second half of the decade, the website plays a vital role in helping the publication hold its own against web-only competition, including popular sites eLuxury.com and shopbop.com. The modern magazine-inspired shopping website, with its increasingly stylish and user-friendly take on e-commerce, may well be the shopping magazine of the future.

The Adaptable Web

In comparison to cable or print, the World Wide Web is infinitely versatile. Any magazine, newspaper or TV station of any consequence has long since established an online version of itself.

Widespread broadband access has done much to speed the web's development as an advertising medium, and unsophisticated pop-up and banner ads have paved the way to more refined ad formats. The "sponsored links" that appear when you type a few words into a search engine are a fast-growing form of online advertising, delivering ads to ever narrower audiences.

While the new media landscape presents challenges to marketers, interactive digital media, especially the Internet, have a couple of important advantages over old mass media. Their interactivity allows marketers to gather a wealth of personal data from consumers and adjust their sales strategies accordingly, even as the transaction is underway. This same interactivity makes it easier for advertisers to measure the impact of their online marketing efforts' impact, from click-throughs to online sales. Advertising clients are partial to the hard figures that web marketing provides.

PERMISSION TO MARKET

According to conventional marketing wisdom, consumers can be identified, communicated with and sold to using traditional segmentation methods.

Looking at the diversity and increasing fragmentation of the North American market, it's unlikely any segmentation formula could fully take into account the variables of our rapidly changing society. Moreover, the segmentation theory assumes target consumers will respond to an ad in a similar fashion, no matter where they are or what they're doing.

Internet technology has given birth to the notion of "permission marketing," or advertising so relevant that consumers welcome it. Marketers have moved well beyond traditional demographics to collect information on people's desires, attitudes and habits. Thanks to advanced data-gathering techniques including phone and online surveys, many publishers offer online and offline content custom tailored to readers' interests.

Micromarketing can be a cost-effective, though not necessarily cheap, means of reaching a specific audience. The narrower the targeting, the costlier the CPM. In addition, micromarketers still need to take great care to manage privacy concerns.

To brand managers that have grown up with mass-marketing, paying more to reach a smaller group of people may seem irrational. But in a world of splintered audiences and fragmented media, micromarketing may prove to be the only effective way to get the message across at all.

In a retail context, matching marketing communications to customer usage occasions can enhance customer loyalty and sales. Going beyond segmentation to consider the frame of mind a customer will be in when she receives a marketing message – including how receptive she is likely to be at that moment – can greatly enhance the effectiveness of an ad or promotion.

The Future of Service

Retailers increasingly need to use their creativity to enhance store environments, offerings and service in order to exceed customer expectations. The store of the future will be filled with contradictions, such as self-checkout alongside personal service provided by sales associates.

Once a customer has entered a store, customer service plays a crucial role in assessing the customer's purpose. Every retailer should have a system in place to help sales associates deliver the kind of experience that will encourage both purchases and repeat visits.

Customer service associates can follow these steps to deliver satisfying shopping experiences to their customers:

Detect and Direct: Once a customer has entered the store, determine her mood and needs, then provide her with the most appropriate service level.

Just Looking: This phrase can be taken as a signal that the customer wishes to explore the store solo. Make it clear you're available to help should the need arise.

Self-Service: Don't press service on customers who want a rapid, no-frills shopping experience. Check occasionally to ensure they're finding what they're looking for and help them complete an efficient transaction.

Standard: These customers may already know the store, and have likely entered with the intention of buying specific items. Make sure they find what they came for, and suggest additional items that might appeal to them. Leave "luxury" items till the end – the purchase of something the customer sees as an indulgence can put a premature end to a shopping spree.

Full-Service: These customers want you to be almost a personal shopper. Feel free to suggest items to them, and help them take full advantage of your store's selection. Make sure they feel pampered and appreciated.

Follow-Up: Differentiate between Self-Service, Standard and Full-Service customers in post-transaction communications.

A one-size-fits-all approach to customer service often fails, because it doesn't distinguish between shopping occasions, and neglects to guide customers in a style appropriate to their mood. Flexible, responsive service is essential to effectively serve and retain customers.

RESPECT THE CUSTOMER

A myriad of technological and social changes have transformed the way marketers view consumers, and the way consumers see themselves. Retail will in turn need to adapt to new realities.

If you want to exceed customers' expectations, it's crucial to get to know them and respect their values. This helps generate enthusiasm amongst your customers, and in your community.

Respect for the customer represents the foundation for the values the retail industry must now adopt.

To succeed, retailers must respect their customers in the following ways:

- **Lifestyle.** Today's consumers are diverse, and individual lifestyle differences must be respected.
- **Time.** Consumers want a fast, efficient, effortless shopping experience.
- **Space.** Give shoppers the distance they need for reflection.
- **Choice.** Consumers wish to tailor their retail experience to their own set of tastes and preferences.

BEYOND SEGMENTATION

Respect for the customer will necessarily be based on a more detailed knowledge of her lifestyle and preferences. Customers these days aren't who they appear to be, and finding out about them will be even more complex in the future:

- **Demographics** and dress cues are no longer useful guides to segmentation.
- **Getting to know customers personally** will help retailers understand each individual's interests, attitudes and needs.
- **Research** will need to gather more intimate information, and find better ways to identify good customers.
- **Sales associates** will play a more critical role in identifying customers.
- **Customer relationship management** will come to mean truly listening to customers to identify their interests and needs.

As long as customer privacy is respected, customers will value retailers' efforts to transform this knowledge into a superior shopping experience.

Customer Enthusiasm

In the future, demanding consumers will expect more from retailers than just satisfaction. They'll expect shopping experiences that exceed their expectations.

- Consumers will want to be repeatedly delighted, so they feel passionate about the retailer.
- Retailers' most prized customers will act as advocates who enthusiastically spread the word about their shopping experiences.
- Consumers can become enthusiastic about innovativeness, freshness in merchandise or store design and in-store events, in addition to a retailer's effective response to their desires.
- Customers don't necessarily want their shopping experience to be defined by the retailer. Customers want to exercise power, defining their own shopping experiences.

Consumers actually crave more opportunities to become enthusiastic about retailers.

EMPOWERED RETAILERS

The disappearance of the mass market, combined with rising consumer expectations, have created challenges for both marketers and retailers. Today's consumer is like no other consumer in the history of retail.

Yet there are plenty of excellent opportunities for retailers and shopping centres that take new consumer realities in stride. Retailers must aim to provide store environments, merchandise, and service that create the ideal shopping experience, communicating these strengths through innovative, narrowly targeted marketing.

Giving the empowered consumer what she wants is no easy task, but the potential rewards are customer enthusiasm and greater relevance in a constantly shifting retail landscape.

By empowering our customers, we acknowledge the changing nature of shopping, and ultimately empower ourselves.

CONCLUSION

SEDUCING THE MODERN CONSUMER

CONSUMERS enjoy greater choice in products and services than ever before. The variety of ways in which people can shop and complete retail transactions has also increased exponentially in the past decade.

The Internet may not have killed the shopping centre, but it has become so integral to our lives that we wonder how we survived without it. Even retailers that do no e-commerce need to understand how the Internet functions as a marketing, customer service and consumer research tool, and how it enables word-of-mouth on a scale never seen before.

Throughout history, technologies that become integrated into people's daily activities are soon taken for granted. Although YouTube was launched in 2005, it is already hard to imagine not having easy access to video clips from any era, on any subject. Text messaging has forever changed the way people communicate, just as social networking sites have transformed how we get to know each other. Much of the future innovation and growth in retail will be the direct result of increased integration between pop culture and technology.

If you ask me whether I feel optimistic about the trends in consumption in North American stores and shopping centres, my answer will be an unqualified "Yes." Consumers remain obsessed with buying the latest and greatest. Many continue to max out their credit cards, putting their old belongings in rented storage rather than putting money in the bank. Our culture embraces consumption and glorifies spending. Borrowing remains a way of life.

North American consumers – be they Boomers, Gen X or Millennials – are accustomed to spending as much as they can to look and feel good. Makeover mania is here to stay. People quickly tire of the things they own, and are forever enthusiastic about changing both their surroundings and their fashions, not to mention enjoying new shopping experiences.

Have we all been seduced by Naked Consumption?

Anthony Russell Inc.

Inspiring Retail Excellence

Anthony Russell Inc. provides detail-oriented and responsive consulting to retailers, shopping centres and organizations worldwide. We deliver personalized service, creativity and cost efficiency without the red tape. Our reputation is based on two decades of giving practical, actionable advice that achieves results.

Practical Insights

Clients receive personalized, in-depth consultation on qualitative consumer research, customer expectation, positioning, branding and strategic marketing. Anthony Russell barters in reality, providing retailers and shopping centres the insights they need to thrive in a competitive marketplace.

Two Decades of Trend Forecasting

Founded by Anthony Stokan and Russell Connolly in 1987, strategic marketing consulting firm Anthony Russell Inc. tracks international trends in every retail category and analyzes every shift in consumer psychology. Anthony Russell works with retail chains, shopping centres and associations the world over.

Keynote Addresses and Workshops

Anthony Stokan has anchored over 1,000 meetings around the world. His keynote speaking is charged with imagination and impact, providing a fresh and informed perspective on consumer realities. Enlivened by recent photos showing retail trends on several continents, his presentations never fail to inform and entertain.

Custom-Tailored Consulting

Anthony Russell provides clients with up-to-the-minute market information, penetrating analysis and tools that help you compete in a saturated marketplace. We conduct custom-tailored strategic audits, facilitate in-house management meetings and identify research opportunities to help you keep ahead of the competition.

Custom Christmas Installations

Show-stopping Christmas décor strengthens customers' emotional connection with a retailer or shopping centre. Anthony Russell specializes in custom Christmas décor packages incorporating a full range of coordinated elements, including one-of-a-kind Santa chairs, gift-wrap stations, and specially-designed trees, wreaths, decorations and lighting.

Christmas Décor Project Management

Anthony Russell handles all phases of the Christmas décor project. Planning services include drawings, prototypes and confirmation of vendors. We supervise production, installation, teardown and storage, ensuring all goes according to schedule. A holiday décor package project managed and installed by Anthony Russell creates the ideal atmosphere for holiday shopping and provides cost-effective, time-saving solutions for management.